SCHEME OF AN IMPERFECT SOCIETY

Historical and political essay on American society

DUKARDO HINESTROSA

ISBN: 9798374295849

Sello: Independently published

Luisa Fernanda Agudelo

Design and layout

Publishing Rights

Credits cover image Collier's Magazine

Every day huge shipments are intercepted by authorities from the sources of origin, as well as on the access routes, but what these seizures do is make the product more expensive and more lucrative in terms of figures.

But since this paradise has its limits, it must be repeated, it is worth it at any cost, for those many are subjected to all the risks, no matter how dangerous they may be, and sometimes they are victims of overdose as they have been stars of entertainment.

In the problem of addiction, there is also in American society, thousands and thousands of patients who depend on opioid drugs, on analgesics to withstand terminal illnesses such as codeine, morphine, vicodin and others, a large legal market, administered by many doctors who turn your prescription pad into a productive way to get rich. The big pharmaceutical houses with their research and vaccine preparation laboratories have become millionaires with pandemics, one, two, three, four inoculations a year, sometimes without being able to stop the scourge.

The artificial paradises of opium, before the arrival in America.

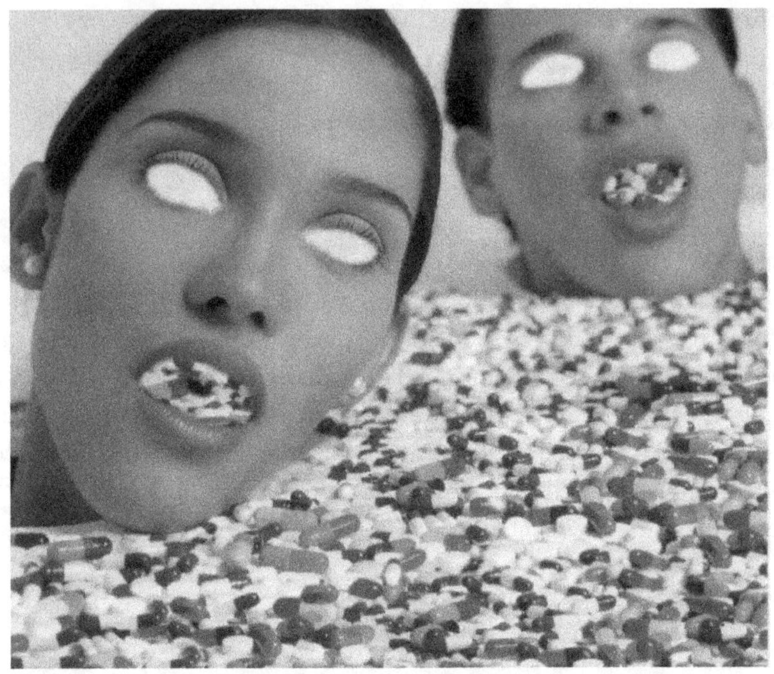

New synthetic drugs.

PRO-AMERICANISM

In all parts of the globe there is great admiration for the American model of life and there are also its detractors for what it is, for what its image represents, especially what it has allowed to be seen through the media, in particular the cinema, TV, videos, internet, speaking of the most positive, there is great curiosity for those who do not know him and for many who have lived him and recognize him as the best in his achievements in all fields.

A supremacy with other Western societies that share with the system, objectives, goals and tasks of overcoming high technology, comfort and security, in addition to competing markets and influences of all kinds. The United States has a number of unconditional friends who follow its statements, have shared its struggles with it, depend largely on its economy and defense, and others who await orders.

Modern technology, fashion, perfumes and cosmetics that used to come from Paris, like the children brought by the stork, now a large part of that market comes from the USA. Many decades ago, the American Union imposed standardized blue jeans throughout the world, which is still in fashion for men and women, automobiles, electronic equipment, chewing gum, baseball caps, filter cigarettes, Hollywood movies, the scandals of his celebrity in weekly magazines and also film, the Oscar results many people have become accustomed to waiting for them in almost all parts of the globe on TV.

The most outstanding characters of his comics: Superman, Batman, the spider man, the bionic woman is frequently recreated over and over again to keep children interested in war actions and the power of the invincible heroes of their fantasy. Indiana Jones, the space adventurers from Star trek and Jurassic Park are still active.

If North America did not have so many restrictions on its immigration services to visit it, its tourists would be in the millions, but it is also terrified of visitors who stay and the terrorism that some criminals who filter in favor of. North America has many things that many would like to come to know, for children perhaps Disneyland and Universal Studios, the great zoos. For adults, natural landscapes such as the Colorado Canyon, Niagara Falls, parks such as Yosemite, Yellowstone, Muir and Sequoia Parks; engineering marvels such as the Golden Gate Bridge in San Francisco, the great Colorado dam, the skyscrapers of New York and its bridges, and cities such as Chicago, Las Vegas, Miami, Los Angeles, Washington its capital, New Orleans, Dallas, Seattle and the mecca of cinema, Hollywood.

The cinema has been in charge of keeping the spirit of the Cowboy alive, with his Texan hat, his pistols and his cowboy boots, presidents such as Ronald Reagan and Lyndon Johnson, kept this outfit not only on their ranches with great pride but also in informal public appearances, his great estates today are highly visited public museums, in Texas and California. Other former presidents have wanted to perpetuate their names with large libraries, where many of their personal effects are kept.

There are a number of people with a fever for everything American, its cigarettes, its cars, its race tracks, movies, its platinum blondes, its porn magazines, its liquor, videos and all the paraphernalia of novelty objects that appear every day, the taste and fantasy that they arouse is undeniable, that many countries copy, repeat and resell them all over the globe.

Donald Trump ruled America as if it were a Las Vegas casino.

THE UGLY AMERICAN: ANTI-AMERICANISM

The hatred that many have against North American society is not completely gratuitous, they have known how to win it with many arbitrariness committed, particularly some governments have collaborated throughout history to fan the fire and try to keep it from going out. In the decades of the 40s, 50s, and 60s of the last century, due to their fear of communism, they propitiated in Latin America the establishment of ultra-right military dictatorships by the majority of nations, which they armed and allowed to enrich themselves in order to open their doors to their voracious exploiting companies of their wealth, also to accept loans to keep them indebted to their banks, in exchange for helping them to remain in power and enrich themselves with their families. Every idea of change, emancipation and shaking off tyrannies by progressive groups was crushed under the title of communists.

This conduct of its agencies, the CIA, FBI and the State Department, managed by inept, ignorant and sinister and unscrupulous characters, propitiated that anti-American hatred. Badly invested money from the beginning, allying with elites who only wanted to keep their people subjugated, ignorant and in misery in order to control them.

What if things had happened the other way around? Helping advanced groups better than outdated feudal structures, promoting the arrival of agricultural machinery in exchange for combat weapons, bringing in technicians in exchange for military advisers, investing capital in education and technology, make loans not to the rich, but to small and nascent industry, promote cultural exchange, share progress in uncommitted institutions, better with the needy, not with the exploiting classes. John Kennedy, with his

Peace Corps program, made an attempt to create a neutral organization to help the peasants above all, but other soldiers advised him to invade Cuba instead. But the blindness of the so-called intelligence groups, managed by sergeants and obscure characters like Edgard Hoover and Joseph Mac Carthy, who saw communists everywhere, even behind the refrigerator, favored a faster feeling of rejection of American institutions and that truly seek in other political ideologies, a more favorable way out.

Another of the agencies created for interventionist purposes was the so-called Casa de las Américas in Panama, bordering Lake Gatún on the limits of the interoceanic canal, where future dictators would be prepared since 1946. It was there that the assassination of President Omar took place. Torrijos, using the ambitious sergeant Manuel Antonio Noriega who replaced Torrijos as leader and was at the same time an agent of the CIA.

The Allen Brothers and Foster Dulles had extensive interference in the Agency to process the fall of Jacobo Árbenz in Guatemala and put the Dictator Castillo Armas. Ranfis Trujillo, son of the Dictator of the Dominican Republic, Leónidas Trujillo, and his son-in-law Porfirio Rubirosa, also the son of Anastasio Somoza, another Nicaraguan dictator, graduated there to continue his father's sinister task. François Duvalier from Haiti, father and son. Several attacks against Fidel Castro and the liquidation of the liberal leader Jorge Eliecer Gaitán in 1948 in Bogotá, at the request of the Colombian elites, were also forged.

Some of the characters, glory and pride of Casa de las Américas who distinguished themselves by their actions and gave it discredit were: Hugo Banzer from Bolivia, Vladimiro Montesinos from Peru, Manuel Contreras from Chile, Roberto d´Abuisson from El Salvador and the tame pigeons from Videla and Galtiere from Argentina. Actors like to make a horror movie directed by Alfred Hitchcock, with characters like Lon Channey and Boris Karlof.

Not all the tasks of the so-called condor operation, thought of in the house of the Americas, most were incinerated so as not to leave a record of so many outrages and errors, when it closed its doors in view of so many complaints against it in 1984, not without graduate almost one hundred thousand soldiers with all their cockades and epaulettes.

Almost obsolete furniture, belongings and weapons were moved to a military center in Georgia. The land where the gloomy house of the Americas operated, of ungrateful memory, was replaced by a luxurious tourist hotel in Panama.

Returning to our account of the great mistakes of many administrations, considered legal and within the normal canons, it has been the Republican leaders who have contributed the most to keeping the flame of anti-Americanism burning, Richard Nixon and Johnson by prolonging the Vietnam War and ignoring the world cry for peace, Bush father and son in his long years of government and his wars in Iraq and Afghanistan and the millionaire Donald Trump, for considering America as a gambling casino where he and his friends always won.

More than a hundred works published by sociologists, philosophers, religious, professors and political scientists are already considered, in addition to many history texts for colleges and schools, pointing out all the mistakes made in the last fifty years. Even in school textbooks they have tried to expose all the mistakes repeated over and over again, but very few learn from these painful experiences. But the ruling classes are not interested in hearing what they do not want to understand, they remain undaunted despite the multitude of criticisms, advice, recommendations that they suggest with the best intentions, they are not going to do anything to change or at least modify a blind policy that is pushing to failure.

But the criticisms or protests do not come from their enemies, a large majority are from their unconditional friends in the West, from those who are on their side, from those who respect them as a nation that shares their world leadership with them. Also, of those who want them to continue exercising a participatory democracy for an indefinite period of time.

En 1972, durante el rodaje de "The Train Bobbers" en Durango, Méjico.

John Wayne: the well-loved American cowboy.

THE IMPOUNDERABLE CRITICISM OF THE NOTABLES

Prestigious intellectuals from all over the world have added their criticisms to North American foreign policy, at different times and in recent times; intelligences of all philosophical, religious and political tendencies such as: Bertram Russell, John Kenneth Galbraith, John Dos Pasos, Jean Paul Sartre, Noam Chomsky, Par Lagerkvist, Graham Greene, Claude Levi-Strauss, Henry Miller, Elie Wiesel, Salman Rushdie, William Fulbright to name a few, several of them Nobel Prize winners, have made important suggestions and comments on his handling of the concept of democracy and how its rulers have applied it.

There were complaints like those of Bolívar, Miranda and Martí, in the early incursions of their expansionist policy, in more recent times, Graham Greene, a British writer considering himself a socialist humanist and at the same time a converted Catholic, was on the side of the underprivileged, in his novel "The Quiet American" published in 1956, alludes to the clumsiness of the US military authorities for their armed intervention in Vietnam and in which he predicted the victory of the Indochinese people, this being a fiction novel. During his last years he focused his theme on Latin America "El Poder y la Gloria", it is set in revolutionary Mexico and his character is a corrupt priest. In "The Honorary Consul" takes place on the Argentine and Paraguayan border, about a kidnapping of the English consul by guerrillas. Greene was a very prolific and successful writer.

John Dos Passos, American writer, author of the novel: USA and other works with overwhelming and devastating prose, by the noisy twenties of the last century, was already a socialist with anarchist ideas, in which he already shared fame. Along with Hemingway, Fitzgerald, Faulkner and others, for him in his golden age international hatred was for the British people, but years later, North America took away his supremacy and he attributed it to the fact that the powerful are always hated.

In responses to his interview with Oriana Fallaci, in 1967 he confessed to her: Poor little Eisenhower was a less than mediocre guy; Kennedy, a complete disaster, was a handsome, friendly Irishman who had a great fascination as a man, but as a president he had no ideas; perhaps, if he had lived longer, he would have been able to combine some things; he had good intentions but until the day he was killed he did nothing but accumulate tremendous mistakes. Now we have Johnson, the personification of the worst political maneuverer devoid of ideals. Compared to them, Truman seems like a great president. Robert Kennedy was a mess, lawless and unscrupulous, he lacked his brother's good looks, in compensation he had all the hateful things of his money-thirsty father.

There is a great lack of skills and to defend ourselves from hatred requires talent, it is the lack of talent that leads Americans to make so many mistakes in the field of international politics, to protect, for example, reactionary regimes and dictatorships. Anyone who is not a socialist is generally called a reactionary. If we were, we should justly agree that America is not reactionary; it entered socialism faster than the Soviet Union. For me the reactionaries are the communists; in my opinion, nothing is more old-fashioned than a communist. There is nothing revolutionary. And I know it well, that in the twenties I was on his side.

Communists as political fanatics closely resemble orthodox Muslims. The American mentality is television, superficial, exhibitionist, based on mass hysteria; if you prefer you can call it the absence of culture. But there are even worse things, our total lack of leaders, with little politicians, without true statesmen.

J. K. Galbraith Canadian writer, statesman and economist, very prolific author, in many of his fundamental works he criticized American armaments and militarism, How to Control the Military, particularly the war on Vietnam and the billions of dollars that were spent and those that will be spent in the future with so-called defense packages. Among his most important works it is worth highlighting: "The Affluent Society", "Economy and Subversion", The Liberal Hour", "American Capitalism", "The Age of Uncertainty" and The New Industrial State".

Bertrand Russell, British philosopher, mathematician, educator and statesman, Nobel laureate in 1950, was a fiery pacifist, was imprisoned several times in protests against the war and repeatedly criticized the policy of the US State Department, author of a hundred works, was also a student of Einstein's theory of relativity.

Noam Chomsky, a professor of American linguistics and a highly controversial author for an important series of theories, recognized worldwide, has been another of the critics against imperialism and the wrong policy of the Pentagon.

William Fulbright, was another notable American statesman who was in the Senate and was a brilliant speaker on politics with the Democratic Party, author with great success of his book: The Arrogance of the Power, criticized Nixon on the abuse of power, the prevailing corruption and US foreign policy and was an opponent of the war in Vietnam and its costs to the public purse.

Years ago, a group of intellectuals from the French left, led by spiritual leader Bernard Cassen, pointed out that the United States has failed to recognize the unpopularity of its policies around the world, not even accepting a revision. As an example, they put the case of the collapse of the capitalist company ENRON.

This stubbornness is what has led to the collapse of great empires. A thesis still valid: "We must not wage war on governments, we must help them to corrupt and they themselves will fall due to their own rottenness." The United States should not worry about the comments of its critics, it should be afraid of its sycophants.

It would be necessary to question the level of ethics and morality of the operating political system, to what extent its degradation has come, how are its bases, if there are possibilities of saving them, what is the vulnerability of the society that governs it in relation to other nations that share their views or no longer see them as worthy of imitation.

It would be good to consult the statistics, how is their level of corruption, of the ruling elites, where is their capitalism heading, which has evolved so much to face new alternatives in the 21st century, if they already consider us an unjust society, based on exploitation of the working classes or our level is so high that it prevents us from seeing the cataclysm where we could rush, which is behind the retaining walls.

How would the philosophers of yesterday, such as Descartes, Voltaire, Spinoza, Kant, Locke, Goethe, Macchiavello, Marx, Smith, Ricardo, Engels, David Hume, Nietzsche, Schopenhauer, look at us and how would they assess the conquests achieved so far? It would be interesting to wake them up from their sleep and sit them down at a round table to talk.

Unfortunately, there are very few philosophers, great economists, eminent mathematicians, illustrious sociologists, noble pacifists, philanthropists, poets who would like to discuss the controversial policy that operates in the White House.

Notable intellectuals and critics of American politics.

John K. Galbraith

Bertrand Russell

Graham Greene

Claude Levi- Strauss

Noam Chomsky **William Fulbright**

John Dos Passos

Par Lagerkvist

MEXICO: OUR GREAT DEAR FRIEND, BUT UNDESIRABLE NEIGHBOR

In the history of North America and Mexico, for many centuries they have been united by bonds of friendship, which to the north resemble barbed wire and to the south a simple cord; A great steel wall has recently been erected, still unfinished in the limits that separate it, in order to discourage the human stampedes of threatening Central Americans who crowd the edge of the border, also demarcated with the help of the waters of the Bravo and Grande rivers, where every day civilians die trying to cross them due to their hazardous currents and deep flow, like a natural executioner, for those who intend to challenge it.

The Aztec nation was one of the largest territories on the globe, like China and Russia, it lacked personnel to take care of its immeasurable borders, which is why it lost much of its geography. The Spaniards first arrived in Mexico in 1519 on the island of Cozumel and later they conquered other territories to the north, years later with their beloved brother from the north they went hand in hand with five states in sales and war, Texas, Arizona, California, New Mexico and Colorado.

The war that lasted two years, 1846 to 1848, was waged by the United States in its interest to annex Texas, a fight that had already begun in 1837 when President Andrew Jackson had already recognized Texas as an independent nation, after this book his battle with Mexico for its separation, for his part the then president of Mexico, Antonio López de Santana, saw these acts as a declaration of war. In 1844, the United States Senate rejected the annexation treaty, but Democrat James Polk, then a candidate, campaigned for the expansionist idea and managed to win the election.

For his part, John Taylor also welcomed the idea in his campaign, until the Congress of the Union adopted it in March 1845. The Mexican government finally, after bitter disputes that lasted several years, accepted several million to end the conflict, in which which included the territories of Arizona and New Mexico with new limits marked south of the Gila River. The cessation of hostilities treaty was called "Guadalupe Hidalgo" which culminated for Mexico with eleven years of war, with its fraternal friend from the North.

YANKEES NO, GRINGAS YES!

The history of conflicts has been very bloody, they are practically two enemies who tolerate each other with immense affection, they need each other despite being so close, the presidents rarely visit each other but business is in order. Every day new Mexicans arrive to live in the north, some across the border with legal papers and others through numerous underground tunnels that exist illegally. There are many retired American citizens who live in Mexico and thousands of tourists who invade their hotels, beaches and tourist sites during the summer.

Relations have not worsened because a large number of American citizens are of Mexican origin, which some contemptuously call them: Pochos, Chicanos, Mojados and individually almost all men are contemptuously called Pancho, perhaps in memory of a revolutionary general who He did a lot of damage to them on the border and for whose head they paid five million after his death, as a museum piece.

Tourism has been a determining factor for the good relations that favor both and the other, the laborers in the fields of agriculture, with temporary contracts, with cheap labor and thousands of other undocumented immigrants. Commercially, treaties have operated with mutual benefit almost all the time.

NAFTA is a free trade agreement that Mexico signed jointly with Canada and the United States in December 1992, between the three leaders of then George H.W. Bush, Salinas de Gortari and Brian Mulroney, having the format signed in Europe, in order to eliminate existing barriers due to bureaucratic procedures and facilitate and speed up negotiations between the three northern nations. The treaty has been surprisingly successful for these three economic powers, creating thousands of jobs and greatly improving mutual friendship.

When the United States manages to legalize the million Mexicans who hope to fix their residency, many things will change.

Warning about anti Americanism.

AN IDEAL DEMOCRATIC SOCIETY IT IS NOT A SIMPLE UTOPIA

The capitalist system as it works now in the territories of the American Union, with its great successes, errors, mistakes, advantages and privileges, compared to other powers that operate in the world, many consider it: Not the best, but the least bad. It could go through many stages of improvement, since a democratic society like the one it aspires to represent is not a simple utopia, it is achievable if it accepts criticism and continues to transform itself into an advanced, democratic, humanistic and generous country.

Its capitalism of the twenties and of the last century is already outdated, I mean the one that Karl Marx and Engels wanted to erase from the map with their ambitious theories of the proletariat. But it has not been an easy path either, it has also cost many victims of several generations; just thinking about what was his awful civil war to end slavery and the hard fight to change those who continue to preach racial supremacy.

The two world wars, their expansionist conflicts, their struggles for a military preponderance over other imperialist powers, their intentions to abolish the intolerance of some communities.

To live in the 21st century, with the advanced technology that we have, which has allowed us to explore outer space and be able to have an orbital station, it was so that we would have already left behind many injustices, intolerances, drug dependency, armament and the pretentious role of being the world's policeman.

The USA will have to make an effort to lead the environmental tasks, forgetting fossil energy, also lead the nations that seek the prescription of nuclear weapons.

Open its borders to a professional, humanist migration and promote special programs to end the adventurism of the search for the American paradise, people who will not contribute anything to progress and rather will become a burden for the state, so that they stay in their countries struggling to improve their homeland in exchange for an uncertain foreign future, committing the Central American leaders who are willing to promote the exodus to focus on their problems of overpopulation.

End the elitist universities and colleges, only for the rich. Democratize more education at all levels, the same sports, managed by mafias.

WELL-INTENDED ACTIONS OF THE SYSTEM

In this compendium and social research, on what the North American capitalist system represents for the world, I want to list some of the most important successes throughout its history, for which it has gained global preponderance:

• Having freed themselves from the oppressive yoke of the British Empire and repudiated its tyranny in 1777.

• Overcame the Great Economic Depression with acts of generosity in 1933.

• Having received a great migration from poor nations such as Ireland, Italy and other parts of Latin America.

• Promote the end of slavery at the end of the bloody Civil War.

• Contribute to defeat fascism, Nazism and other totalitarian systems in the Second War of 1945.

• Having received a large number of victims of world conflagrations.

• Denounce the ignominy of the Berlin Wall and help destroy it. 60s decade.

• Help nations economically, to overcome problems of underdevelopment.

• Deliver to Panama all sovereign rights over the isthmus canal.

• Maintain permanent vigilance with societies that proclaim white supremacy.

• Grant a series of aid and social services to the community, social security, unemployment, disability, retirement funds, hospitalization and others such as Welfare.

• Cover the expenses of global catastrophes and assist them with emergency personnel.

• Maintain an open immigration service for new applicants to residents.

• Assist with funds and services the humanitarian programs of the United Nations.

• Sponsor with economic funds educational programs such as scholarships and specializations for students from poor nations.

• Fund satellite space programs with other nations for scientific research.

• Collaborate to make possible the development of shared sports.

• Make possible the existence of Red Cross hospital ships that serve poor and needy patients in other continents.

• Make possible the democratic game of periodic elections and curb the ambitions of candidates who wish to perpetuate themselves in power.

• Collaborate with Civil and Human Rights Organizations.

• Financing medical care for Pandemics such as Covit 19.

• Abide by the determination of the Courts of International Justice.

• Amendments and reforms to the laws to update them and make them fairer.

• Having created programs such as The Peace Corps and The New Deal.

• Grant scholarships and make financial aid possible for poor students.

• Generously humanize immigration systems.

• Control more the repression of the police forces with the citizenship.

• Maintain a democratic game without political proselytism, anti-totalitarian.

HERE COMES THE PLAGUE

"Here comes the plague, he likes to dance

And when she's rocking out, she owns the place".

Latin rock.

"Plague, disease that affects a large number of people".

Larousse dictionary.

In the year 2022, people have received up to a fourth vaccine, the last two are considered reinforcement to stop Covit 19, however there are a large number who, despite being vaccinated, have contracted the virus, which proves that there is still a long way to go experimentation.

Just as in the Middle Ages (15th century), appeared in Europe: The Black Death that decimated the world population in many millions of human beings, almost 50%, due to the bubonic plague, caused by the rat flea, of In the same way, in 1918 a terrible Influenza appeared that in America was given the name of Spanish Flu, and that quickly spread throughout the world and whose victims reached 22 million, it is said that the contagion was brought by some soldiers who They came from Africa, the continent that the Bible speaks of where the seven plagues of Egypt originated, plagues were frequent at the time of Moses and Pharaoh. Since then, pandemics have been considered a punishment from God.

The marine combatants who arrived by ship in North America were already sick and soon infected their families, the government had to take extreme measures in all public buildings and the use of surgical masks was mandatory and anyone who coughed was expelled or isolated. Influenza, just as it appeared, disappeared too.

Other serious diseases have been smallpox, a highly infectious virus that appears with skin rashes and was already present nine thousand years before Christ. Polio, which usually appears in childhood, was suffered by Franklin Delano Roosevelt until his death in 1945. SARS appeared in Asia and spread to more than 30 countries.

AIDS has been terrible for America, a problem due to immunodeficiency, coming from Africa, it is said that the first cases date back to 1920 in the Congo and on the railway where the workers of the diamond and precious stone mines were transported most contagious in Haiti in 1964, where it was detected, passed to America and has caused a large number of victims, there is no vaccine to date.

In recent years COVIT 19 has been the most dangerous virus, due to the ease of its contagion that has been decimating the population in the states of the American union, it is rumored that it came from China, in recent years. The vaccines arrived late when it had already claimed numerous victims; the scourge is now worldwide and the number of victims already exceeds six million.

The necessary information on how to stop the virus still does not exist, the measures taken to prevent contagion have caused great economic disasters and the stress caused by the restrictions of the health authorities, have intensified protests in many nations creating social instability worldwide. Although collective vaccination at all levels has apparently slowed down the contagion, the variants of the same disease continue to be very dangerous.

The latest plague that is giving a lot to do is Monkeypox, which is characterized by boils that appear all over the body and is very contagious in 2022.

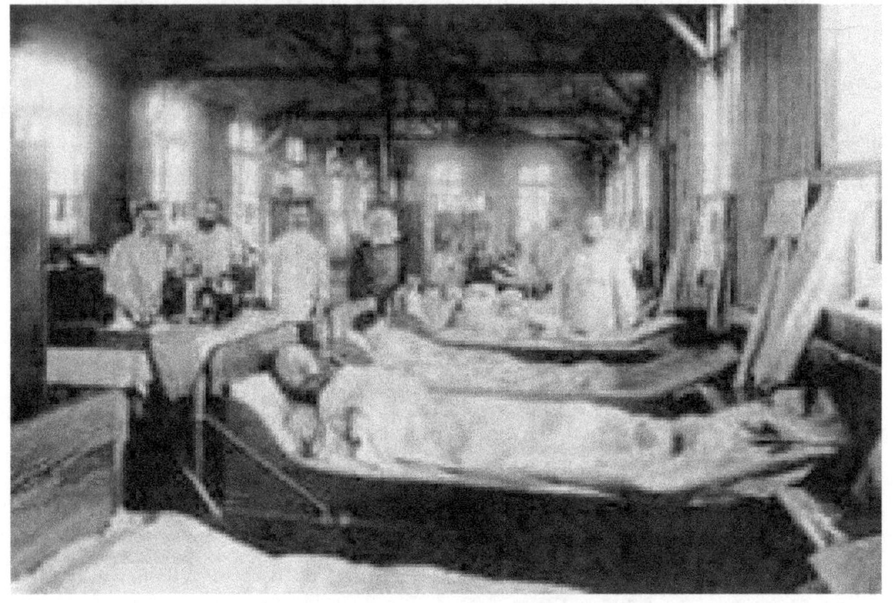

Cholera Pandemic (1881-1896).

THE HIPPIE GENERATION: HUMANIST RENAISSANCE

Although many do not want to see it that way, the hippie generation that emerged in North America in the 60s and 70s constitutes the most important pacifist social movement of the 20th century, which shook the structures of the establishment, as a result of the great crisis that the nation experienced with its bourgeois behavior and its materialistic capitalism focused only on success. The interesting thing is that it emerges in a time of great changes and transformations, after the two world wars and the expansionist interest that arose in a ruling class that sought to become a voracious and insatiable imperialism, as was England.

At that time the existentialist and defeatist philosophy was wreaking havoc in post-war Europe, desolate and spiritually hungry. The works of Jean

Paul Sartre, French writer of the time, who in 1964 rejected the Nobel Prize and author of works such as: El Ser y la Nada, La Nausea, Critique of Dialectical Reason, whose obligatory and influential reading was absorbing the thought of youth, full of anguish, doubt, desolation and not they saw a way out in the alternatives of authoritarian Soviet imperialism and a dehumanized and decadent materialist capitalism.

In America, the emerging hippie generation of a white middle class begins to feel the need for change, alien to the predicates of the Status Quo and without the political primers of a messianic prophet, dissatisfied with everything that was unfolding around them, and without practicing violent acts, proclaiming love.

The generation of 1950, The Beatniks who preceded him, had left him nothing but an intellectual legacy but with some anarchist alienation, full of doubts and despair like existentialism with "The Howl" (Howl), by Allen Ginsberg, the novel bohemia of Jack Kerouac's “On the Road”, the iconoclastic ideas and the angry verses of other prophets such as L. Ferlinghetti, Gregory Corzo, William Burroughs, Peter Orlovsky, Neal Cassady, Bob Kaufman, Luden Carr, but at the same time with the search individual liberties, human and civil rights. The post-war philosophies of angry and outraged existentialists also greatly influenced the behavior of the Beatniks.

The hippies adopted other paths more in line with the philosophy of Epicureanism, Hedonism, simplistic ideas and angry protest like that of Diogenes the cynic, named for his extravagances, and living in a barrel; Lovers of friendship, peace, beauty and return to a simplistic, contemplative, uncomplicated life, setting aside modernism, the canons of fashion, luxuries and the laws of success. Her downside was mind-blowing drugs like LSD and marijuana that made her very vulnerable.

Woodstock, a psychedelic Rock music festival, scheduled in New York at White Lake Park, on Monday, August 15, 1969 and which lasted for three days, was its launching pad. An event with a grandeur like never before in the world of entertainment. Almost half a million hallucinated young people, half naked and defiant, opposed to the reigning conventionalism, anarchic and willing not to continue with the established capitalist model

They refused to go to war, publicly burned their draft cards, and began practicing free love in parks, finding great refuge in hallucinogens, marijuana, LSD, and other stimulants. "The Teachings of Don Juan" were his gospel, the Yaqui Shaman who taught about the hallucinogenic virtues of peyote and who introduced Carlos Castañeda as his initiate. Later, other enlightened prophets appeared, such as Timothy Leary and Albert Hofmann, who led phantasmagorical and hallucinatory trips with psychedelic formulas in search of artificial paradises.

For the hippie youth, living in the improvised commune, out in the open was the new ideal, sharing food, drinks and cigarettes was already the norm. Striking rock was the most explosive, jazz, blues and country music, listening to the Beatles, Jefferson Airplane, Jimmy Hendrix, Janis Joplin, Carlos Santana, Tijuana Brass, The Papas and The Mamas, his greatest entertainment, Joan Baez, Bob Dylan and his pacifist songs, the itinerant, nomadic life, moving like the gypsies, with long hair and wild beards, barefoot or in light sandals, working a few hours, without avoiding raising children.

The hippie movement: The Flower Children, or Flower Power, as many called it, was seen without the negative mitigating factors, because it was from young white people, who preached peace and love and did not have confrontations with the forces of order, only until he actively joined the pacifist movement, and made his cause his own, against the Vietnam War from 1954 to 1975. In some times other religious groups took advantage of them to take advantage of proselytizing, such as the Hare Krisnas, who came from India with some Gurus Introduced by the Beatles, the "Jesus Movement" also emerged, a group of religious youth who sought to change the hippies and guide them in the religious tasks of Christianity. The presentation of the work "Jesus-Christ Super Star" caused a stir, the image of Christ as a Rock Opera star, in the Age of Aquarius and the end of the Mayan Calendar.

As a great coincidence, mysterious by others is "The Age of Aquarius" that appears in the zodiacal calendar of astrologers and that brings with it a series of omens about great surprises for humanity, every two thousand years and that will last until 2060. His arrival was well received and motivated many artists to develop an artistic work to leave a positive message to future generations in America. With the name of ACUARIUS, a musical work was presented that had great preponderance, both for the theme and the work of the actors, following the message of the Hippies of love and friendship.

The Generation of hippies, just as it appeared, also disappeared, but it will always be remembered for the creative passion it unleashed, helping to discredit the architects of the Vietnam War, with a pacifist message of love and brotherhood.

His gray, dark and negative part also had it with the crimes of Charles Manson and his hippie family, he really overshadowed the entire generation with his satanic, chilling, perverse and murderous image and his trial served to denigrate an entire Era of hippie love. Another very negative message was also the film EASY RYDER, starring Peter Fonda and Denis Hopper, the bohemian life of two motorcyclists, with a sad, violent and overwhelming ending.

Like the capitalist consumer society, The Establishment, considering it an affront to the system, rejected hippie society, and never valued messages of love, friendship, peace and brotherhood, he did everything possible to present it as something that would not be repeated, because it was not convenient for him, he preferred warmongering, commercialization, the search for success, as the maximum expression of what man should have as a goal. The system channeled it back into the channels of the status quo to the following generations, trampled on its flowers, erased its messages, shaved its hair, imprisoned a large majority and made fun of its legacy and its statements, but since everything is repeated and the life is a circle like The Eternal Return, a philosophical conception postulated in written form by Stoicism as a cyclical fact: see the ouroboros ancient Egyptian symbol in the circular form of a worm, serpent or winged dragon that begins by devouring itself with its own tail, with the Greek inscription the one, the whole, that according to the rules of Hermes Trismegistus of the esoteric principles, that the human future has a beginning and an end that will lead us to perfection with the passing of time. Also supported by Federico Nietzsche in his work "La Gaya Ciencia", a return of the society of peace and love is possible in times to come.

In the hippie society of the 70s, long hair and the African-American style prevailed

The author at the time of the 60s.

New Hippie Generation in the 1970s, America had a major humanistic renaissance.

SEX AND SENSUALITY IN AMERICAN SOCIETY

In the development of the great community, through all its epochs, sex and sensuality have been kept as a secret ceremony, restricted many times by religion and by the moral and ethical precepts implanted by the very society in which we live as great sins, some with numerous taboos. Something that does not happen within what we call animals or wild, particularly among mammals that move and practice sex naturally, without reservations as an urgent call of instinct, without feeling shame and guilt, for the sake of preserving nature species. The only rule that prevails in some groups is the so-called mating season, where nature allows females to be more willing to allow the encounter and tolerate the demands of the male. Generally, in their reproductive parts there is a musk that encourages penetration. In the deer it is known as the bellowing season, a favorable time for hunting.

Humanity, on the other hand, or animal man, is moved by other behaviors and different behaviors that have become very sophisticated over time, except for what they call the cave age, the film industries have done something, to give us an idea, and how it was that erect Pithecanthropus, Rhodesian man, Neanderthal or Cro-Magnon made love.

For North America, its sexual awakening begins in the fifties with the appearance of a Playboy magazine, its founder and editor Hugh Hefner, an ambitious young man who knew how to interpret the need for a change in the conservative bases on sex and sensuality and the moral and religious customs of the union; his first copies catapulted him as an icon of sexual liberties, the themes were very suggestive and well cranished and his nudes were very explicit and artistic and millions quickly arrived in his bank account from a society grateful for his efforts in liberation of the old and stagnant taboos.

Gloria Steiner did something similar with her magazine Ms. in 1972 with numerous articles that helped to create an awareness of sex, to use condoms and women's politics and to demand their rights in a time of turmoil due to social problems, at the same time I actively participated in organizations for civil rights and in the search for better job opportunities and for women to put aside the jobs of housewives and prepare in colleges and universities to share positions in the official bureaucracy with men and in private companies.

One of the most important contributions on sexuality in America is due to the psychologist and entomologist Alfred C, Kinsley, who in the 1940s and 1950s became one of the pioneers of research on behavior and the conduct of society. North American with several studies and reports that updated a series of existing problems, topics considered forbidden and untouchable even in schools and colleges about sex with adolescents.

Freud became fashionable with his questions couch, Darwin too, an opportunity that Hollywood took advantage of to introduce Lolita and platinum blondes charged with eroticism, massage clinics proliferated and Dionysian paradises.

Cinema and television owe much to the great opening of sensuality in the American Union, increasingly explicit, after ending censorship, magazines and weekly tabloids appeared in the advertising media, to which was added the scandals of the artistic celebrity, politicians and celebrities of the film artists revealed by paparazzi, opportunistic photographers who persecuted them to surprise them in compromising moments. Diana the English princess was one of his victims, while fleeing, a victim of his harassment.

Celebrities of the film industry were: Shirley Temple, Judy Garland Marilyn Monroe, Hedy Lamar, Jane Mansfield, Carole Lombard, Lupe Vélez, Raquel Welch, Jessica Alba, Nathaly Wood, Rita Moreno, Marlon Brandon, Tony Curtis, Clark Gable, Tyrone Powers, James Dean, Anthony Perkings, Fashions, cosmetology, cosmetic surgery and continuous changes in search of new incentives to maintain youth and beauty, have made gyms prosper and a great paraphernalia of instruments and aids to make sculptural lines more noticeable.

In recent times with the acceptance of gay marriages, a great opening has begun for the acceptance of transgender people by defining their sex and their public manifestations. At the beginning of the 21st century, there have been numerous changes in social life and its behaviors, dammed for many centuries, not long-ago cloning was considered a great alternative, in the same way the manipulation of fetuses in the gestation stage, the change of sex, the stimulants and aids to obtain more pleasure and prolong the periods in the sexual rite or ceremonies. At this point there is little left to increase and innovate when it comes to sex; North America is one of the countries that sets the standard, to follow and imitate it.

The Hippie society of the past half century was definitive for a great opening of the union of free inter-racial couples, without the ties and responsibilities of marriage commitment. Now what sets the tone is fatigue, tiredness, routine and the need to experience new changes and emotions. Parents today accept this tolerance with their children who turn the home into a motel.

A current problem is the regulations on abortion that have kept society divided, when what they should really worry about is preventing unwanted pregnancy, with so many condoms and contraceptive methods on the market, which should begin in schools, colleges and in the home itself, where false morality and ignorance have always prevailed. Abortion would not exist, with campaigns to prevent pregnancy and make the use of condoms more accessible, more information and classes on sexology are needed. A positive fact that must be taken into account in modern US society is a series of laws in favor and protection of women, in which Latin America is still far behind, as is the African continent. Machismo continues in black and Latino neighborhoods, where violence and family conflicts are more frequent.

Hugh Hefner had a lot to do with sexual liberation for several decades.

AMERICA FACES THE NEW 21ST CENTURY

The beginning of the 21st century for the American Union, presented itself with a very flattering and optimistic panorama, finished the nightmare of having to confront the Soviet Union with its totalitarian policy of Marxism, and an imminent atomic war of rockets with nuclear warheads, equally with China, supposedly the two potential enemies. Thanks to Glasnov and the Perestroika implemented by the Kremlin, the second important step was the dissolution of the Supreme Soviet and that of these nations adopt free enterprise and end the indoctrination policy of a single party, with the primers of Mao, Marx and Lenin.

The United States had nothing to do with these changes, nor the FBI, nor the CIA, nor the Pentagon, they arose from the very need to evolve towards a better society, nor were there revolts in its proletariat, the conditions and changes simply arose emerged due to the need to avoid stratification.

With this nightmare of communism, which terrified the republican party so much, without having to fire a single shot, thanks to Mikhail Gorbachev's policy of openness and his desire to give more oxygen to the suffocating structure of the official Moscow government apparatus, the The US Department of State quickly applauded the measures taken by the Russian president, congratulating him and giving him the support he needed to finalize the necessary changes, since in some sectors of the Kremlin, such as Boris Yeltsin's, great concern was arising from this shake-up. of their bases.

It was not a matter of dismantling socialism, but of loosening the nuts of a rigid party machinery, adopting the policy of: supply and demand, to alleviate the long-standing economic crisis, reduce censorship and at the same time, develop a new dynamic with a great opening of Free Enterprise, which would benefit a large number of small entrepreneurs. Also give the nations of the Soviet bloc the opportunity to grow alone, without the rigid tutelage of a single authoritarian party.

China was the most benefited from this policy, it put aside Mao's primers and dedicated itself to doing big business with all nations, offering ample and new credits and invading the markets with attractive products, starting with Latin America.

Nor was there a class struggle in the Chinese giant, nor were there protests from its proletariat, there was simply a need to open a gap to its isolationism and seek markets for its growing mercantilism and mega-production. But suddenly the picture darkened with the arrival of Los Estudiantes; name translation: Taliban in Afghan terms. No one thought that a leader like Osama Ben Landen, who was trained by the American armies and helped with money and weapons when he was fighting against the Russian invasion in Afghanistan, suddenly decided to confront the colossus of the north for a long time, it's great and generous supplier, and lined up its batteries with a satanic and mephistophelian intelligence, planning a series of terrorist acts against the United States that first began in 1993 with explosions in the World Trade Center in New York, then it was at the American Embassies in Kenya and Tanzania in 1998, to finish with a flourish with something spectacular, something that would shake the conscience of the American and the Western world, he spent four years preparing something that would truly demonstrate the vulnerability of the Colossus of Capitalism, considered until then impregnable territory.

On September 11, 2001, the twin towers succumb to the crash of planes hijacked by the Taliban bonzes, planes with passengers on domestic flights became suicide kamikazes, the pentagon and other bureaucratic dependencies were the target that were programmed in the diabolical plan of Osama.

The result I imagine satisfied the fevered mind of Muslim terrorism, 3,000 dead and thousands wounded. Since then, the term terrorist has been officially enthroned, practically replacing the term communist that used to terrify so many Americans.

Suddenly everything changed for North America, the Pentagon intelligence realized that in a few hours a Saudi Arab, without such great power, had shaken their bases and had sent their president flying for hours looking for the best hiding place, it was no longer a war of Marxist politicians, the one he had to face, but the feverish hosts of the Prophet Mohammed, ready to make those they considered infidels and enemies of the Islamic faith disappear.

The manager of the satanic odyssey went up in smoke, he was also looking for hiding places everywhere and for a long time, changing places, but like Hussein, the FBI sleuths finally found his lair and like a cornered beast, an elite of Marines, he was no longer looking for him to prosecute him but to liquidate him with bursts of M 47, and all this duly televised with a limited face-to-face audience in the White House, while they consumed Popcorn, white popcorn.

An exaggerated protectionism in airports and a series of uncomfortable security measures have made the life of the majority of ordinary citizens, but terrorism has also globalized and each country now has a contribution of victims at the hands of religious fanatics.

But not everything has been fatalism for the American Union, with the arrival of the digital era, telephony has invaded all fields, everyone, particularly young people, women and children are seen with their cell phones. The internet and the multimillion-dollar proliferation of active computerized tablets have stolen attention from problems as serious as the environment, the melting poles and uncontrolled temperatures, the little pocket wars in a world plagued by excesses.

THE INTEGRATION OF ETHNIC GROUPS

A very interesting phenomenon to consider in today's modern American society is that of the integration of races, creeds and customs, until forming a homogeneous conglomerate that has been erasing differences, with interracial marriages that were previously considered impossible due to segregation, now Putting for example the case of attending a baseball game, before the audience was mostly Anglo-Saxon, now the images have been modified there are Asians, Latinos and blacks, enjoying a sport together, which was previously predominant for whites, other sports such as football and tennis. Movie theaters and other outdoor shows are integrated.

Pizza is already devoured by all ethnic groups, the same as Mexican tacos and burritos, as well as hamburgers and hot dogs, they are preferred in the so-called fast food. Undoubtedly, restaurants, theaters and stadiums have been the predominant places to achieve integration.

An annual spectacle that the whole world is already waiting for is the Oscar ceremony, decades ago reserved only for whites in the film industry and that now begins with a fashion show on the red carpet, now it is a function integrated by all races and the musical show is very varied.

The Churches have been slow to integrate, violent acts against them no longer occur and the racist formula of the 3 KKK seems to have definitively gone into recess. The ghettos have also calmed down and an apparent peace now seems to reign.

The Immigration Department has been very active, it has a lot of work to do, there are many thousands of citizens waiting to naturalize, thousands more in the process of legalizing their residence, and deportations also have a high margin in official statistics. In the south of the United States, Latinos, the majority Central Americans, have been the ones exerting the most pressure to join American society. Big cities like New York, Los Angeles, Chicago, and Miami are the most racially integrated.

In the state of Florida, due to its proximity to Cuba, it will have to be 100 years since the Castro revolution, in order to heal the division of two Cubas and two Havanas and for the new generations to face the issue, leaving behind the bitterness of the first exiles, affected by the socialist measures of nationalization and the exchange of currency carried out by Che Guevara, when he was economy minister, leaving without funds the Cuban dollars that rich businessmen brought to Miami in their suitcases when they had to leave the Island unexpectedly.

The idea of the two Cubas will also have to disappear when the Castro surname is nothing more than a legend and the idea ends that there could be no socialism without them, and that the island was a family heritage, as Somoza thought with Nicaragua and Trujillo. With the Dominican Republic of wanting to perpetuate himself in power with his entire family and offspring.

The integration of ethnic groups may also occur when the white race in the American Union becomes a minority and with the votes it is surpassed by Latinos, which is the ethnic group that increases the most every day, followed by the black and Asian races. This is going to happen when the immigration department legalizes the millions of Latino citizens who are waiting to be recognized as residents and who now live in a stationary limbo. Similarly, the growing number of residents who acquire American citizenship and are allowed to vote within the traditional parties.

It is important to keep in mind that the census forms do not consider Latinos as white even if they are blond, it is enough that they speak Spanish for them to change color to Brown.

The so-called bronze race has modified the demographics in America, according to data from the last census in 2020 it is the fastest growing, while the so-called white race has decreased. Would it be interesting to know, in what race category are the children of a blonde woman with a black classified with the new multiracial integration, according to the criteria of the census officials? By 2022, the North American population was considered to be 330 million, a very significant growth with a white population of 45%. On other continents the white race is alarmed at how it is being overtaken by other growing ethnic groups.

An existing problem is that the race considered as supremacy does not recognize the corresponding legal percentages of power to grant to other ethnic groups; the votes in the elections should be the ones that count when choosing officials for your bureaucracy.

In cities like Los Angeles, a predominant factor are the areas where certain communities with inhabitants and businesses are grouped, that is why there are white Beverly Hills, Chinatown, Korea Town, Japanese Quarter, the Mexican East, Watts to the south of blacks and sectors from Central American, Vietnamese, Afghan, Armenian and Filipino.

THE ARBITRARIES COMMITTED THROUGHOUT HISTORY

• Make war on Native Americans to dispossess them of their best lands.

• Establish slavery in the southern states, and thus prolong their emancipation.

• Promote racism, make lynchings and practice the supremacy of the white race.

• Despite having such a large territory, continue with an expansionist policy.

• Fight the native tribes and want to annihilate them in all the states of the union.

• Discriminate against minorities and force them to speak only English.

• Bomb Hiroshima and Nagasaki with atomic weapons.

• Massacring workers on strike, who were seeking better wages and job guarantees.

• Download Orange chemical bombs, napalm and incendiary bombs in Laos and Cambodia.

• Destabilize democratically instituted governments.

• Promote military dictatorships and help them with weapons and ammunition in Latin America.

• Create repressive organizations to carry out political espionage.

• Sell weapons to reactionary and criminal dictators and satraps.

• Allow pollution and exploitation of energy products from fossil fuels.

• Make punitive incursions internationally with political motives.

• Allow brutal repression of some police groups.

• Give budget priority to the manufacture of weapons, then to education and health.

• Having waged a war against Vietnam, committing so many atrocities

• Allow the glorification of violence in film, television and videos.

• Continue with the policy of legalizing weapons in homes.

• Support high-priced elitist Universities and Colleges.

• Accept that sports are managed by millionaire mafias.

• Consider nations that think differently from us to be enemies.

• Pretend that we are the best in the world and that we do not make mistakes.

• Give away destructive weapons to fuel wars.

• Be very generous in times of internal economic crisis.

IMPORTANT DATES IN AMERICAN HISTORY

1607 Arrival of the first English settlers in America, Chesapeake.

1620 Landing of pilgrims on the Mayflower.

1754 War with the native Indians.

1769 The first steamboat is patented by James Watt.

1773 Boston Tea Party war action by colonialists against England.

1776 Revolutionary ideas are promoted with the book Common Sense, T. Paine.

1776 Declaration of Independence.

1776 Adam Smith writes The Wealth of Nations, founding El Capitalino.

1783 Treaty of Paris ends the American Revolution.

1787 Constitutional Convention in Philadelphia.

1791 Bill of Rights, added to the Constitution.

1800 Manifest Destiny, the expansionist idea is put into effect.

1800 The first labor unions or unions begin.

1800 Clark and Louis begin exploring the American West.

1812 war between the United States and England,

1814 Treaty of People, ends the war.

1820 Wall Street, The Stock Exchange begins activities in New York.

1830 The Abolitionist Movement gains strength.

1830 Native American tribes are relocated from their lands.

1836 Texas War for Independence.

1846 War with Mexico for the annexation of Texas.

1848 The gold rush begins in the American West.

1848 The struggle for women's rights and suffrage begins.

1853 Alaska by purchase becomes a Union territory.

1854 The mafias in New York begin their criminal history.

1858 Conflicts and struggles for and against slavery in Kansas.

1861 Civil war begins.

1865 President Abraham Lincoln is assassinated.

1881 President James Garfield is assassinated.

1886 Massacre of workers in Haymarket Square in Chicago.

1892 New York's Ellis Island opens its doors to immigrants.

1895 Radio is invented.

1898 The war between the United States and Spain begins in Cuba.

1899 William McKinley begins his term as president.

1901 President McKinley is assassinated

1908 Henry Ford launches his first model car.

1909 The NAACP Negro Movement is organized.

1914 The First World War begins.

1919 The Treaty of Versailles is signed.

1919 The dry law begins, prohibition of liquors.

1920 The Roaring Twenties, The Jazz Age, begin. The Roaring Twenties.

1920 Anarchists blow up the J. P. Morgan Bank in New York.

1922 Benito Mussolini brings out his first hordes of fascists.

1922 The Union of Soviet Socialist Republics is organized in Russia.

1922 Washington initiates the Teapot Dome scandal with President Harding.

1924 Ellis Island, near the Statue of Liberty, closes its doors.

1929 Great Depression, Stock Market crash, economic crisis.

1930 Aviator Amelia Earhart, first to cross the Atlantic.

1933 Liquor prohibition ends.

1934 Enrico Fermi discovers the elements of uranium for the atomic bomb.

1939 Amelia Earhart disappears in an attempt to go around the world.

1939 Black and white television begins to function.

1940 The Second World War begins to ravage Europe.

1941 The Japanese empire attacks the American base at Pearl Boil in Hawaii.

1944 General D. Eisenhower leads the assault on Normandy, France.

1945 The medicine industry produces the first antibiotics.

1945 The United States drops atomic bombs on Hiroshima and Nagasaki.

1945 Japan and Germany surrender, World War II ends.

1945 The United Nations begins activities.

1949 NATO is organized as a defensive pact.

1950 The so-called Cold War practically begins.

1950 Republican Senator Joseph MacCarthy initiates fascist tasks.

1950 The conflict with North Korea begins.

1953 The Rossemberg couple are tried for spies in favor of Russia.

1954 Segregation in schools is declared unconstitutional.

1955 The so-called Warsaw Pact is born.

1957 Russia jumps ahead in the space race by launching its first Sputnik.

1958 The United States launches its first Explorer satellite into space.

1961 Kennedy orders the Bay of Pigs Invasion in Cuba.

1962 Astronaut Alan Shepard makes his first orbital flight.

1962 Political crisis over the nuclear platforms in Cuba.

1963 March on Washington by Martin Luther King Jr.

1963 President John F. Kennedy is assassinated in Dallas, Texas.

1966 The NOW Women's Movement is organized.

1967 Three astronauts die in the space vehicle.

1968 Martin Luther King Jr. Leader of the blacks is assassinated.

1969 Walk on the moon, by astronaut Neil Armstrong, Apollo 11.

1969 Half a million soldiers sent to fight in Vietnam.

1972 Democratic Party offices stormed on Nixon's orders.

1973 American troops leave Vietnam.

1974 President Nixon is forced to resign.

1975 Vietnam is unified, after the surrender of the southern military.

1986 Scandal of Iran Contras in the government of Ronald Reagan.

1989 The Berlin Wall falls.

1991 Glasnov, ends in Russia, the Union of Soviet Republics.

1993 Islamic extremists detonate bombs in New York.

1994 NAFTA Trade agreement with Mexico and Canada.

1998 Al Qaeda terrorists kill 258 at American Embassy in Kenya.

2001 Al Qaeda attacks the twin towers in New York.

BIBLIOGRAPHY

TITLE	AUTHOR
El Talón de Hierro (The Iron heel)	Jack London
El Capitalismo del Pentágono	Seymour Melman
El Capital: Critica Económica	Carl Marx
La Coexistencia Pacífica	F. Lerroux
La Formación de la Conciencia Burguesa	Groethuysen, B
Los Derechos del Hombre	Auger, P.
Encantamiento y Magia	Castiglione, A.
Ideología y Utopía	Mannheim, K
Teoría de la Clase Ociosa	Veblen, T.
La Riqueza tras el Poder	Brady, R. A.
Estudio de los Grupos	Klein, J.
Historia del Pensamiento Social	Barnes, H. E.
The Power Elite	C. Wright Mills
The Money Game	Adam Smith
The Weapons Culture	Ralph P. Lapp
The New Industrial State	John K. Galbraith

Poder Negro: Política de Liberación	S. Carmichael
Zona Sagrada	Carlos Fuentes
La Revolución Teórica de C, Marx	Louis Althusser
La Rebelión de los Machetes en América Latina	Dukardo Hinestrosa
La Fabula del Tiburón y las Sardinas	Jacobo Árbenz
The Affluent Society	John Kenneth Galbraith
Democracia en América	Alexis de Tocqueville
Soul on Ice	Eldridge Cleaver
Democracy and the Public Service	Frederick C. Mosher
Five Lectures	Herbert Marcuse
One Dimensional Man	Herbert Marcuse
The Naked Ape	Desmond Morris
The Rise of America	Theodore Roosevelt
La Revolución Permanente	Leon Trotsky
The Century of U.S. Capitalism in Latin America	Thomas O´Brien
The Politics of Experience	R.D. Lang You
You Shall Be as Gods	Erich Fromm

El Miedo a la Libertad	Erich Fromm
The ABC of Relativity	Bertrand Russell
The Handy History Answer Book	Richard Hofstadter
The Limits of American Capitalism	Robert L. Heilbroner
Listen Yanqui	C. Wright Mills
Our Depleted Society	Seymour Melman
The Pentagon	Clark L. Mollenhoff
Kennedy	Theodore Sorensen
The Silence Weapons	Robin Clarke
Intervention and Revolution	Richard Barnet
A History of the Twentieth Century	Gilbert Martin
American Catholicism	Ellis, John Tracy
Up from Slavery	Washington, Booker T.
The Killer Angel	Shaara, Michael
The Radicalism of the American Revolution	Wood, Gordon S.
El Laberinto de la Soledad	Paz, Octavio
Revolución en la Revolución	Regis Debray
Desarrollo Económico Acelerado	Lauchin Curie
Apra Rebelde	Víctor Raúl Haya de la Torre

Las Venas Abiertas de América Latina	Eduardo Galeano
La Rebelión de los Pueblos Débiles	Antonio García
Petroleo y Politica	Ernesto Frondizi
Oil and Revolution in Mexico	Brown, Jonathan C.
Race and Manifest Destiny	Horsman, Reginald
Filibusters and Financiers	Scruggs, William
The Economy of Death	Richard J. Barnet
The Wealth of Nations	Adam Smith
The Birth of The Nation	Arthur Schlisinger
Sin Novedad en el Frente	Erich María Remarque
Another Country	James Baldwin
Decline of the West	Oswald Spengler
State of Denial	Woodward Bob
Waste Land	T. S. Eliot
El Largo Camino a la Libertad	Nelson Mandela
Porque No Podemos Esperar	Martin Luther King Jr.
El Nacimiento de Una Nación	Edmond Sears Morgan
The Killer Angels	Michael Shaara
Up From Slavery	Booker Washington
Ideas y Opiniones	Albert Einstein

Historia del Dinero	Jonathan Williams
Roots of War	Richard J. Barnet
The Protestant Ethic and The Spirit of Capitalism	Max Weber

ILLUSTRATIONS

All images were taken from the author's private collection, which was acquired throughout his life. The original source is unknown.

The cover design was in charge of Dukardo Hinestrosa and Luisa Agudelo.

Credits cover image *Collier's Magazine*

CONTENTS

WORKS BY THE SAME AUTHOR

GAITANIA REVUELTAS
ROSARIO y FUSIL
DUKARDO HINESTROSA
NOVELA

Cancionero
Folklórico
de Colombia
DUKARDO HINESTROSA

esen
EL SENDERO
DEL ESEN
DUKARDO HINESTROSA

THE WAY
OF THE ESSEN

"DEMOCRACY NOW"

Returning to the case of the formation of this society with immigration "The Melting Pot", it continued to grow in the twenties of the last century with the arrival of thousands of Irish as a result of a time of famine suffered by this nation where for a long time the daily menu consisted only of potatoes so as not to starve. North America opened its doors to them.

The Irish have distinguished themselves since time immemorial for their conflictive nature, they made their homeland a permanent territory at war, and it was they who, upon arrival in the new world, organized the first criminal mafias, later they were supplanted by the Italians who found a field already paid due to problems of overcrowding, lack of work and old criminal family clans.

THE PROMISED LAND: LA TERRA PROMESSA

When a great wave of ragged Jews arrived at Ellis Island in New York, amazed at everything they saw, many of them believed that they had finally reached the promised land that Abraham and Moses spoke of; moved by the beautiful New York panorama, after so many persecutions, the biblical exodus had ended long before the United Nations handed over the territory of Israel in old Palestine. Of course, the panorama was not very flattering, overcrowding in old buildings, unsanitary conditions, famines and great danger in the streets, but the Jewish people were noble, grateful and received everything with great resignation. They were not going to be alone; the neighborhood was to share with other Irish communities and with others that were already on their way.

Although the great Jewish community was organized with a nationalist movement since 1882, it did not become a reality until 1948, Zionism was focused on the lands of old Palestine in the Middle East, and Southwest Asia; in the limits of the Mediterranean Sea, also bordering Lebanon, Syria and Jordan. The term Zionism was taken from Mount Zion, a place in ancient Jerusalem, where the Jewish community had erected the Temple of David, in 962 BC, as its spiritual center. Now there is only one huge wall left that they call the Wailing Wall, where they come every day from everywhere, especially Jewish pilgrims to pray.

As a political movement, Zionism is said to have been founded by an Austrian Jew named Theodore Herzl in 1890, well known for his involvement in the notorious Dreyfus Affair.

The territories assigned to the great Jewish family in the state of Israel, remain conflictive areas, claimed by Palestinian Arab families, it is practically the same community with two religions, Jewish Christian and Muslim, where there is a permanent state of anxiety and belligerence. Israel is very well armed, thanks to the permanent help of the United States and had a war with Egypt during the time of Nasser.

As for the Jewish community that settled in America, before they were given their territory in Israel, many came to stay and it has been very prosperous and rich. Some of the great personalities of the Jewish world who came to settle at that time were the scientists Albert Einstein and Robert Oppenheimer. Other Jewish personalities who went into exile were Sigmund Freud and the philosopher Ilia Ehrenburg.

In 1939 the Ship Saint Louis with 907 of the Diaspora of Jews, their request to enter Fort Lauderdale Florida was rejected and they were sent back to Europe, some were saved, but most died in the Nazi concentration camps.

During the convulsive period of 1850, in Italy what was called The Unification began to be forged, almost thirty million took the path of exile to different parts that had better possibilities to live and the American land was the one that had the resources to receive a great migration, with all the problems that this community suffered, residues of what was a great empire many centuries ago.

Numerous families arrived from the South of Italy, with them also came to New York, elements of the Camorra, La Mano Negra and other Mafias, establishing an empire of horror for its way of operating. Hollywood has glorified them with numerous blockbuster movies. Who does not remember Alphonso Alcapone "Scarface", in the days that turned the streets of Chicago into battlefields with the rattle of activated machine guns from luxurious cars in motion? It seems incredible, Alcapone was not prosecuted for the crimes he committed, only for not paying taxes and sent to Alcatraz. The then Minister of Justice Ramsey Clark referred to it as the most powerful private organization in the world, which were initially known as bandit "gangs" that operated in isolation, sometimes united only by "La Omerta", a law that silence and a close fellowship of solidarity prevailed, but there were only about 30 families that controlled a few thousand criminals.

In the existing records and files of the New York police of 1870 and 1880, the term "Mafia" did not exist, but the word "Dago" did exist, to disparagingly mention Italians and Spaniards, as well as the word "Cafoni", applied to vagrants, marginalized or criminals.

The statue of liberty was a gift from France

L'A ITALIA CRIMINALE

James McCabe, author of the book "Lights and Shadows of New York Life", describes that chaotic happening in the dark streets and suburbs of Latino neighborhoods, controlled by roughs, rudos or highly dangerous ruffians, who took advantage of the prostitution, drugs, gambling, white slavery in the port area, many of its victims appeared floating in the waters of the Hudson River. But there was a way to buy protection from Los Piccioti, young people recruited by the mafias. In Chicago, Italians lived in worse conditions, crammed into the working-class neighborhood like a can of sardines, in old buildings that threatened to collapse; by then the population increased from five thousand to five hundred thousand, most of these ghettos were infected by rats, tuberculosis and syphilis, ravaging the elderly. Begging was another scourge within the community.

One of the Latin newspapers, L' Italia, founded a protective organization for Italians. The city of Chicago was governed at that time by a don "boss of bosses", a criminal tycoon who was the one who elected the prefects, his name Michael Casius McDonald.

There was so much crime and the extortionist gangs of La Camorra, La Mano Negra and Cosa Nostra, that the Federal Immigration Control Commission suggested closing the borders for those arriving from Italy, although the community attributed the existing problem to a fusion of several races, although it was known that there were numerous families from La Calabria and Sicily, southern Italy, who fought among themselves for the control of criminality.

Las Vegas Nevada became the gaming capital with its casinos and large hotel centers, where the new controlled mafias have given free rein to their recreated dreams of Don Corleone and Scarface, Lucky Luciano, Sam Giancana, Anastasia Genovese, Frank Costello, F. Galluccio and others. Las Vegas was the city where Peter Lawford made mob contacts to help finance Jack Kennedy's campaign, which involved Frank Sinatra and Judith Campbell Exner's female contact.

By the year 1920 the government did not pay much attention to social problems and the proliferation of these ghettos, it only cared about collecting its taxes and corruption was at its peak with police that turned a blind eye. But those who best tell the story of their entire career among the so-called Maffiosi, are themselves, one of their most important historians was: Nicola Gentile, who in turn was one of the most important Capos, and said that each city of Los the United States had two or three important families that controlled the activities of the members of Cosa Nostra, which almost covered the entire national territory. But Hollywood with directors, actors, producers and very well-informed people from Italy, have been the ones who have recreated with great poignancy the most sinister episodes of that fight between their families. Mario Puzzo with F. Coppola with the story of The Godfather, they created a masterpiece.

We must also recognize that from Italy we received a great contribution of all its Renaissance art; writers, musicians, painters, singers, actors with all the best of their histrionic talent, covered a cycle of many carats that is still in force. The virtuous legacy of Enrico Caruso, Tito Schipa, Mario Lanza, Salvatore Bacaloni, Renato Carasone, Luciano Pavarotti, of actors such as: Rodolfo Valentino, Vitorio Gassman, Ugo Tognazi, Marcello Mastroianni, Giancarlo Giannini, Al Pacino, Robert de Nero is still recent, Ugo Tognazzi, Franco Nero, Alberto Sordi and others more triumphant in the Hollywood firmament.

From beauties like: Pier Angelli, Silvana Pampanini, Silvana Mangano, Sofia Loren, Ana Magnani, Claudia Cardenali, Elsa Martinelli, Monica Vitti, Lucia Bose, among others. These beautiful divas brought joy to the sad panorama of cinema, fashion and entertainment, not only with their scenic art, but also with their voluptuous erotic and sensual message.

From directors such as: Vittorio de Sicca, Roberto Rosellini, Luchino Visconti, Alberto Lattuada in recent years with the theme of the Maffiosi,

Francis Ford Coppola, we must also recognize other geniuses such as Martin Scorsese and Sergio Leone.

In the field of literature, in addition to the classics such as: Dante, Petrarch, Virgilio, L. Pirandello, there were also the adventures of Emilio Salgari, Rafael Sabatini and more recent authors such as Carlo Collodi, Alberto Moravia, Umberto Eco and an important generation that have fed the hunger of film producers, such as Giovanni Guareschi, author of The Little World of Don Camilo. A communist priest, a humorous version that had a great following for several years. Luigi Barzini has recreated for the world the image of the Italian with all his hair and signs with a fresh narrative abundant in rich nuances that make his descriptive task in The Italians very entertaining.

Like any migrant community, of white people with great traditions and a proud past, in New York, Chicago, Boston, San Francisco, Italians, while respected, were greatly feared since 1920, entire families who came from the southern part of Italy and from islands like Sicily and Calabria, they exterminated each other for the control of criminality.

Among the most famous: Alphonso Al Capone, Salvatore Maranzano, and Frank Costello. John Gotti, Lucky Luciano, Vito Genovese, Jin Colosino, Tomas Gambino and Johny Torrio, most of them already dead or serving sentences. [1]

During the reign of Lyndon Johnson, the mafia was considered almost a second government, controller of hallucinogens, a well-paid market, prostitution, illicit gambling, weapons, and kidnapping. It was widely rumored that he financed the campaign of John Kennedy, Frank Sinatra in his best years, as a singer and actor, became a link to obtain funds.

Havana before Castro was the center of operations in all the Atlantic Islands for large illicit businesses, controlled militarily by Fulgencio Batista with large casinos, too many brothels, very visited on weekends. The monarch at that time was Carlo Gambino "Capo de tuti Capi". The

[1] In a short time, they became as powerful as the already existing companies of Standard Oil International, Texaco or General Motors, according to the chronicles of that time.

debauchery, the corruption made the island the biggest brothel of those times, the result: The Revolution.

In the 1920s, large human waves also arrived from various nations in Europe, Asia and the Middle East, from the Caribbean islands, particularly through Ellis Island in the New York Harbor section of Manhattan.

It is considered that at that time about fifteen million entered legally, the majority were men, the sick was returned. Ellis, the island converted into a port of entry, was owned by the merchant Samuel Ellis, the government acquired it in 1808 as a defense fort and of approximately three acres, but it was only until 1892 that it was given the character of a port of entry with some forty buildings next to where the Statue of Liberty is located. The immigration service was terminated there in 1924 and today it is a place of great tourism as a historical monument.

In the southern part, neighboring Mexico, for many decades the United States has received the largest flow of Hispanic immigrants, particularly at the time of the Mexican Revolution, many fled north as a result of the bloody conflict. Due to its difficult to control extension, the United States has used all the time the cheap labor of the so-called: braziers for its crop fields with a system of renewable contracts. Unfortunately, new technologies and the use of modern machinery in agricultural fields have left many workers unemployed.

The communities of Chinese, Japanese, Filipino, Korean, Vietnamese, who have entered because of wars and other economic motivations. Today they are communities very prosperous and have been integrated into the American union system as a great workforce.

The Crucible of Races continues to grow every day. Due to wars, new residents have entered the country from everywhere, where the United States has become involved. From Cuba and the Caribbean there are millions, nobody forgets the so-called: Marielito's. From other countries that have had war and political conflicts as exiles, El Salvador, Guatemala, Venezuela and Nicaragua, have requested temporary aid. In the year 2021 another large number from Afghanistan, 30,000, have started arriving in the thousands. For their part, waves from Central American countries such as Haiti and

Honduras are preparing to run the luck of being admitted.

The United States has been generous with those who have served it and has established a system of raffles and annual fees for their admission. Your Immigration Services have been kept very busy legalizing new people and deporting illegals every day. With the students they have been given a gracious opportunity to finish their studies.

The most used weapon in America: The pistol

Lucky Luciano **Al Capone**

THE ANARCHICAL MOVEMENTS

"The passion of destruction is a creative passion."

Bakunin.

Along with economic growth and industrial development, social struggles came to play a preponderant role, and with them the first workers' organizations and unions in defense of their interests, influenced by numerous political theories, which sought to catechize them for their cause with revolutionary messages, including Leninist Marxism. In the guild and union of transporters, corruption was present during the time of James Hoffa, of Irish origin, the mafia was in charge of eliminating him after Nixon, before leaving the White House, pardoned him.

Anarchism, communism, fascism, liberalism and other isms began their tasks in a fertile field for agitation within the nascent voracious capitalism of that time. Italians, Irish, Russians, the most politicized, led strikes and demonstrations that collided with the forces of order, which became less tolerant and more aggressive, many were expelled from the country and others imprisoned. Nicolo Sacco and Bartolomeo Vanzetti who had emigrated in 1908 from Italy, two anarchists were accused of having stolen funds for the payment of wages from a shoe company: Slater Morrill Shoe, $15,776 dollars, in whose assault two of the tellers and security guards died.

Almost a month later, the two anarchists were arrested, without further evidence, processed in a quick trial, they were considered guilty and were sentenced to the electric chair; there were many requests for forgiveness, including the Pope at that time, but the pleas were ignored and the sentence was carried out, what the authorities were looking for was a scapegoat to intimidate the frequent actions of the agitators. Years later, the former governor of Massachusetts and presidential candidate in 1988, Michael

Dukakis, claimed the honor of Sacco and Vanzetti.

Anarchism in 1920, as a philosophy at that time, had some very flattering and convincing statements and principles: "Individuals must be free and no one should try to govern them, governments have used violence to establish themselves, they are unjust and illegal, no government is good. It is said that anarchism has its foundations in Chinese Taoism or also in Greek Stoicism. In the French Revolution an anarchist movement arose that was called Les Egaux or in Spanish, Los Iguales, which intervened a lot in the trials. Its philosophers such as Bakunin and Henry David Thoreau continually criticized the industrialists of the time, the latter with his work published in 1866: Civil Disobedience.

In North America the Calvinist pastors William Godwin and Pierre Joseph Proudhon became famous for implementing Anarchism, but this was not just an intellectual philosophy, it was very combative, it was also the noisy time of The Roaring Twenties, and the banners proliferated with the slogan: Live anarchy! They intended something similar to what was the taking of the bastille in Paris in the French Revolution, guillotining bourgeois. The anarchy that his followers supported at that time, did not seek to establish a new government or authority, on the contrary, that there would be no government, no laws, no taxes, no tax tasks, but full freedom for all. But in this type of society, with a great mixture of races and customs, what would appear would be a great general chaos.

Anarchy reigned in Spain for a long time, but its fruits unleashed great violence and the result was catastrophic, fascism, the Falange and Francoism, after a prolonged civil war, the prelude to the Second World War.

In Italy, Benito Mussolini in his long political career, started it as an anarchist in 1919 to create great chaos, generate social discontent and finally ended up creating Fascism, a remedy worse than the disease: totalitarian government with a single party, authoritarian and not tolerant of opposition such as Nazism and the Spanish Falange.

The term anarchist for many, became a symbol of violence, instability, disorder, civil disobedience and chaos, quite the opposite of what its founding philosophers wanted of a great society with many freedoms, without ties and chains.

The anarchist term in the West was changed to communist, terrorist or Taliban, on the opposite side, as in the Soviet republics, the derogatory term was bourgeois, counter-revolutionary or fascist, to label those who opposed the system.

DEMOCRACY IN AMERICA: AN INTRICATE MODEL TO BUILD

The political structure of the North American system, as it is currently made up, is a veritable labyrinth of pieces to put together, some do not fit with others, others seem to be left over, while in the total conglomerate there seem to be missing pieces, however the framework reveals at a glance that they are not made to the same measure, a puzzle with unequal figures that politicians arbitrarily move.

It also resembles a game of chess with a king and queen who would be their elites, their horses the troops and weapons, the subordinate official bishops, the rooks their urban properties and the pawns the working class, as for the board their great territory and the squares perhaps their states, the game would be the political moves of their parties or rulers.

It could be a large patchwork quilt, with its multicolored pieces like the ones grandmothers used to create in their spare time, and the finished work would represent today the nation with irregular parts of democratic concepts, patchwork of dictatorships or authoritarian governments, anarchic movements , human rights, religious concepts, slavery, individual freedoms, plutocracy, supremacy, racism, liberalism, autarchy, chaos, militarism, vagaries and a thousand others, which have resulted in what we represent today to the world.

Great philosophers influenced its structures: politicians in their paths, soldiers in their triumphs and defeats, economists in their bases, heroes in their rights and freedoms, jurists in their laws and a great varied and homogeneous migration of inhabitants that make up its melting pot. The product is not finished, it continues in constant mutation, the day it becomes static it will fall due to its inertia.

Adam Smith, Ricardo, Keynes, Malthus gave it its capitalist foundations, Bakunin shook its structures, Washington, Jefferson, Adams, Franklin, Hancock gave it its freedom, Lincoln abolished chains, Franklin Delano Roosevelt saved it from economic chaos, Ford, Rockefeller, Morgan, Carnegie made her rich, Al Capone criminalized her, Edgar Hoover and J, Mac Carthy undermined her democracy, Nixon and Agnew embarrassed her, Obama glorified her. Over the course of so many decades, there have been many names that have contributed to exalt it before the world and a few more to disgrace its institutions with mismanagement and want to turn it into a family patrimony to get rich, distorting its principles and spoiling its prestige.

THE INDUSTRIAL REVOLUTION

It was in the last decades of the 1700s and the beginning of the 1800s, when the so-called Industrial Revolution began to be born in Western Europe, particularly it emerged with great impetus in Great Britain, one of the most powerful nations converted into a growing empire, later it would go the colonies of America such as the flourishing United States of America, with the use of steam engines and their transportation with railroads and ships, which also motivated a great exodus from the countryside to the big city that demanded a large workforce. 150 years ago, they had great preponderance, as it was the leading freight and passenger transport railway for the development of the industry and progress was vital.

Some knew her as the noisy black woman, who entered whistling, emitting vapors and gases, especially she began in Utah, Ohio, Baltimore, Maryland, Washington, Virginia with different names such as Union Pacific, Pennsylvania belonging most of the time to private companies for the civil war, it was important, because in it many armies were mobilized, blacks and whites were their machinists, the robber barons controlled it for a long time. In Europe they have had more development with the new Bullet Train models.

Large manufacturing factories appeared that gave way to growing technology, with them full employment for the manufacture of weapons for the first world war and later for the second with ships, tanks, planes, rifles, machine guns, bombs, cannons and a large number of weapons. Ammunition paraphernalia. Henry Ford with his automobile factories, is recognized worldwide and recognized even by Nazi Germany that came to decorate him; together with Nelson Rockefeller they become industrial magnates.

The Industrial Revolution undoubtedly constituted a great transformation of an economic nature for the so-called great powers or nascent empires, because at the same time a great technology was developed and gave way to modern inventions in all fields and reached an enormous preponderance already entered the century. XX. The wars were a source of foreign exchange, of great profit for the manufacturers of weapons of mass destruction such as long-range rockets, battleships, submarines, tanks, flying fortresses, cannons and the nascent nuclear weapons.

Along with industrial development, an aggressive, brutal, materialistic and dehumanized capitalism is also being forged in America where working days lasted more than twelve hours, where children were treated equally as adults, but wages for them they were few coins; deaths were in the thousands, especially in the coal mines. In the urban sector, the large factories and sewing workshops were managed by despotic foremen who demanded higher performance to satisfy the bosses in their accumulative desire, the government was an accomplice of these practices to keep the nascent corporations happy.

This was the capitalism that Karl Marx and Frederick Engels knew, against which they lined up their batteries. The interesting thing was that it all started in London, the capital of the Empires, where the so-called "Dialectical or Scientific Materialism" was cooked to great boils. Marx spent many hours studying the behavior of ants and bees, he saw them as proletarian societies, the queen as a monarchy and the drones as bourgeois who lived by exploiting the worker bees.V. Lenin was also in London preparing his machinations against the Tsar of the Russians, Nicolas Romanoff with a certain tolerance, something that he could not do in his country.

The British capital was an experimentation laboratory where philosophers, scientists, warriors, religious, politicians and prophets such as: Karl Marx, Lenin, Gurdieff, Ouspensky, Blavasky, Krisnamurti, and Annie Besant with her astrology and Theosophy, ventured into implanting their theories of moment.

THE DEVELOPMENT OF CAPITALISM

"Founding a bank is a more serious crime than robbing it."
Bertolt Brecht

In America, within the nascent and voracious capitalism in formation, the great robber barons, Robber Barons, operated with their banking platforms which they called Wildcats Banks, that is, with an official license to operate their businesses with leonine interests, backed by armies for the case that Delinquent Debtors arise.

The derogatory term of Gentlemen Thieves, was used for a long time in Europe, also with some who charged taxes on the roads as a toll, in Germany they were called Raubritter, but it was used with usurious lenders who charged high interest rates in America.

Some renowned figures such as J. Pierpont Morgan, John D. Rockefeller, Jay Cooke, Andrew Carnegie, Cornelius Vanderbilt and Edward H. Harriman among the most notable, who knew how to take advantage of the favorable circumstances of granting loans to the nascent nations, with their corruption of ruling military and also of a flourishing national trade with enough cheap labor, especially of recently arrived immigrants and taking advantage of the philosophy of: Laissez Faire, that is, without any interference for the private sector. The great Barons with the backing of Washington rapidly increased their fortunes and by their meddling in politics, made the path easier and more unobstructed for their voracious purposes.

While the nascent empire was being refined in America, entities such as Morgan's emerged, of a banking type with large international tentacles to the concentration of monopoly-type capital, a faithful copy of the guidelines of other world empires with the merger, in addition to political forces, the defensive support of a militarism willing to follow orders and invade any territory that is late in its payments or with nationalist plans. With the same surname, Henry Morgan the English buccaneer, who ventured into the Caribbean in Jamaica, Haiti, and Panama became very famous with his pirate raids, managed to defeat the Spaniard Alonso de Campos and take away his loot. The Monarch Carlos II, awarded him the Order of Knight for his intrepid actions, a distinction that was awarded to another pirate, Francis Drake.

Keep in mind that a select group of American millionaires created their charitable foundations in order to financially help institutions, this gesture by some members of their ruling elite has shown that their spirits have been permeated by a feeling of altruism and philanthropy including Andrew Carnegie, Rockefeller and Ford.

Today some one hundred families of the most notable and rancid lineage, make up the economic elite of the American Union, including that of Rothschild and Donald Trump, a large part of them within the Republican party and from which most of the candidates to run the country.

Based on the fact that China and Russia abandoned the proselytizing struggle with the primers of Mao, Marx and Lenin and adopted: Free Enterprise, in a short time they have been taking over international markets, in Latin America imports and exports have skyrocketed in billions, markets that practically only the United States controlled.

The external debt that Latin American countries have with the United States reaches trillions of dollars, their dependence is increasing instead of decreasing, now China has also entered particularly as a lender and the figures are increasing.

Cornelius Vanderbilt

John D. Rockefeller

Jay Cooke

Andrew Carnegie

Andrew Carnegie

J. Pierpont Morgan

THE SHAKING AND PULLING ECONOMIC HEART: WALL STREET

Internationally recognized in the world of finance: The New York Stock Exchange, had its origin in May 1792, the throes of the 18th century, but its official recognition was only made known in the city of skyscrapers in 1825, a few blocks from the gothic structures of the mansion of God: Saint Patrick, located in old Manhattan, the most expensive place per square centimeter in the financial world and for which they paid the native Indians in colonial times $50 dollars for the entire island.

There are the business papers of the richest and most powerful entities in constant fluctuation of values. The transactions begin, not with an Our Father, as our first fathers of the country would have wanted, but with the blow of a hammer, followed by the vociferous electronic hubbub of thousands of computers, in terms of frightening and numerous figures.

But not all the wealth is there, if we are going to talk about heavy gold bars, these are piled up for square miles like building bricks in Fort Knox, in the state of Kentucky, a large military base with a layout of streets and avenues, which are illuminated with the yellow light of physical gold, despite the fact that they no longer support the value of the dollar. An English philosopher, perhaps Bertrand Russell, if I remember correctly, noted the contradiction involved in excavating thousands and thousands of tons of rock, pulverizing it to extract the gold and then burying it again in deep underground: "It comes out of the earth and returns to the earth".

Gold is no longer the financial support for the issuance of bills, things changed with the Republican Nixon, who changed it for oil "black gold", which is said North America has another large billion in liters in available deposit, until the reign of fossils ends.

Several times the little street Wall Street has been nervously congested, as in the years of the great depression, when several tycoons, victims of despair due to the economic disaster, opened their skulls with a Smith & Wesson in 1929. The street also some poets have mentioned it metaphorically in their songs, García Lorca, Evgueni Evtushenko and two other bards from the black continent.

The economic disaster or great depression of the so-called Black Tuesday on October 29, 1929, which lasted until 1939, affected banks, finance houses and real estate investment entities, as well as foreign banks; its domino effect dragged not only tycoons but also small businessmen and other countries, creating a panic, which forced many to withdraw their funds in savings and that they received devalued; there was a great discouragement for the nascent capitalism politically it had a lot of impact, that some came to think of anarchism, fascism and other isms as a solution.

Of course, there were a number of causes, which were determining factors for the depression to occur, for example: Overproduction, limited participation in international markets, due to debt from wars, lack of liquidity, lack of preparation for the crisis. Unemployment reached impressive levels such as 16 million unemployed with a consequent famine.

Wall ST- Street in New York

NEW DEALS

Emerges as a saving formula in 1933, during the period of the second Roosevelt Franklin Delano, who floated a generous policy: "The new deall", full of good intentions to try to solve the deep economic crisis that was beating the nation, the president began his term with a formula that moved the country: "The only fear we have to fear is our own fear."

He began his tasks with a series of substantial reforms, creating new sources of work, establishing protectionist institutions, which the Republicans derisively criticized as if it were Alphabet Soup. Lines to receive a bowl of soup stretched for several blocks or simply to get an apple, something unprecedented in the history of the economic capital of the world.

Unleashed the Second World War, there was a great demand for weapons material with the consequent full employment and the economy was recovering. One of the great contradictions of the nascent capitalism was finding in war a powerful incentive for development, the automotive industry had a great boom and the defensive system such as bomber planes, tanks, cannons, submarines and ammunition of all kinds. As a participating nation in World War II, which was precipitated by the cunning ambush of Japanese imperialism at Pearl Harbor: the night before the attack, Japan deployed a fleet of 33 ships two hundred miles from the US base with 300 bomber planes, which began their macabre work on December 7, 1941, shortly before 8:00 A.M. in Hawaii. Days later, on December 11, the nation officially entered the world contest.

The United States woke up from a great stagnation and entered fully into the conflict with its consequent contribution of victims. The wife of the president, Eleanor Roosevelt, had a great performance in social and conciliatory tasks, she was his second right-hand man during the entire presidential period that was cut short with the surprise death of the president in 1945.

Franklin Delano Roosevelt

Eleanor Roosevelt

MANIFEST DESTINY
NATIVE AMERICANS AND THEIR STRUGGLES

General George Armstrong Custer, June 25, 1876.

The native Indians, despite firearms, won many battles against the army.

A large part of the religious communities of Puritans and Quakers, recently established in America, took advantage of the opportunity to seize arable land from the natives with the criterion that what they were doing was approved by Divine Providence, and that it was a mandate from heaven, besides, the tribes were savages who had no soul and were other animals, like buffalo or caribou, there was no sin in these incursions. Thousands of them from different tribes were dispossessed of their territories by cannon fire and rifle fire, giving way to what was called: The Trail of Tears, The Trail of Tears, where approximately four thousand died, including women, the elderly and children, victims as well of endemic diseases.

With these actions, the religious leaders began to support the legend that their expansionist ideas were the will of the Supreme Creator and that the first states of the American Union had been anointed by divine will to appropriate all the territories they wanted, with the healthy purpose to bring civilization, religion and progress.

The indigenous communities that originally populated large areas of North America, limited themselves to living in secular backwardness without major concerns of wealth and improving their standard of living, for many centuries, the conquerors, although they were cruel and bloodthirsty with them and They snatched their best lands, it was the way they established new civilizations, cities and towns.

There were battles like the Tippecanoe in 1811, when General William Henry Harrison defeated the Shawnee Indians, then the persecution with the Sioux Indians whose chief Siting Bull, Sitting Bull, joined by another Indian chief Crazy Horse, fought to keep their reservations against General George A. Custer, with whom they fought the greatest battles and managed to defeat him, then withdrew to Canadian territories and five years later returned to their old territories in North America. After they were marginalized in controlled areas, they established a certain tolerance that is still in force. Many tribes survived in isolated regions to which they were confined, now called reservations, preserving their dances and traditions, without the persecution of those who wanted to erase them from the map.

In other territories further south, the Mayan, Aztec and Inca cultures lived isolated for many centuries, it was found that they were advanced societies due to their remarkable architecture, arts, astronomy and agriculture. They had their own calendars superior to that of the Spanish, the Gregorian calendar.

Only human sacrifices were reasons to consider them savage, but those who declared themselves civilized not only killed those they called infidels, but also tortured them before killing them with their call: Holy Inquisition and Holy Office.

Spain did not civilize, it syphilized all the territories where it was leaving an execrable legacy of contagion. In the Spanish caravels many diseases arrived from Europe that did not exist in the New World, during the disembarkation routine hundreds of rats sneaked in that brought the bubonic plague, a large number of ex-convicts from prisons came sick with syphilis and gonorrhea.

Many of the indigenous communities in North America armed

themselves and learned to handle the war material that was confiscated from the English settlers. Thousands died in these contests and the wars became more frequent and bloodier, and as was obvious the native Indians were eventually evicted from their settlements and forced to exodus into inhospitable areas. Over the years these territories took the name of reservations.

It is considered that 60 percent of the native population was decimated in a very unequal war, even the buffalo, and their source of survival, were also almost annihilated. Over time, these punitive actions were seen as a mandate from God, and that the northern country was predestined to govern the destinies of as many territories that were within their reach and wanted to conquer, this was the thought of some leaders in 1800.

In other times and latitudes, something like that, it was written in many ancient Jewish biblical texts that the people of Israel were predestined to govern the territories they could control. In this way the expansionist and slavery idea arose that many imperialisms put into practice, also based on similar campaigns such as the Egyptian and Roman empires of using war to annex and subdue nations.

In America, it all started with the acquisition of the French territory of Louisiana. In 1819 it was Florida and the narrow area of Alabama and Mississippi, which was then called the Old Southwest and was acquired from Spain with the Adams Onis Treaty. In 1845 it was the turn for Texas, after the bloody battles that this territory waged to become independent from Mexico when it longed to become a free and sovereign nation due to its great extension, in order to become a member of the American Union in a short time.

As early as 1846, its borders became closer to the west, between Canada and what is now the territory of the state of Washington. With the Guadalupe Hidalgo Treaty in 1853, southern Arizona purchased the so-called Gadsden Purchase from Mexico, thus completing the rich state extensions to the south.

At the international level; Manifest Destiny is invoked and justified again in the War against Spain in 1898, at that time Cuba was waging its struggle for independence against the Spanish Empire, led by the illustrious poet José Martí, who was offered arms by the government. American, but worried about not falling into the clutches of the expansionist desire of the United States, he rejected it, so the imperialists used a well-prepared dark stratagem, blowing up one of their ships that was anchored on the Cuban island, giving a reason enough to declare war on the Iberian Peninsula and be able to claim its colonies as compensation: Philippines, Guam, Puerto Rico, Cuba, Virgin Islands.

In 1903 it was the case of Colombia with its Panamanian territory with the economic collapse of Fernando de Lesseps, who abandoned the idea he had started of making an interoceanic canal like the Suez one, when his economic coffers reached rock bottom, Teodoro Roosevelt, then President of the American Union, offered the conservative government of Colombia to buy the rights to finish it, but since they opposed it, the astute president promoted a meeting of notables from the wealthy Panamanian families and proposed a Machiavellian plan for them to become independent from Colombia and offered protection, in case the government intervened. By then Roosevelt already had a large navy ship anchored in the harbor with soldiers ready to disembark; Colombia in those years was engaged in the so-called War of a thousand days, a political contest between its two parties, Liberal and Conservative, everything was consummated in a few days and the jubilant Panamanian people proclaimed their independence. The Colombians had to resign themselves and accept a handful of dollars as compensation.

In the case of Cuba, when it was struggling to free itself from the Spanish yoke, the United States offered to help Martí with weapons, but he, afraid of falling into the clutches of the voracious empire, rejected it. However, the explosion of an American ship gave him reason to declare war on Spain. The triumph of the nascent North American empire gave it the great opportunity to annex other territories held by Spain during its conflict with the Iberian Peninsula as spoils of war: Puerto Rico and other Caribbean islands, as well as the Philippines, Guam, the American Samoa, Hawaii, Midway and the so-called Virgin Islands. Cuba had to accept the American occupation for three years, after having liberated itself from Spain. The voracity of the nascent empire perplexed the overseas empires. In a short time, the geography of the United States was almost transformed into the American continent, there was no longer any territory from north to south where they did not have interference and control.

In the territories acquired by all means, discontent grew since in order to control them they committed many outrages, awakening in them a liberationist idea against the new masters. Puerto Rico created a new nationalist party, led by Albizu Campos, with the purpose of shaking off what they called "New Tyranny", in which an attack against President Harry S. Truman was presented, in which both were killed. Parts. However, the new masters were rich and generated progress in all areas, something that never happened with the Spanish dependency that only cared about looting them authoritatively and keeping the populations under religious obscurantism.Many see the idea of Puerto Rico becoming independent from the United States with a great nationalist and patriotic spirit, but in reality, a large majority prefer TIO SAM, a rich and powerful uncle, to living like any poor and backward Latin American country.

The democratic and progressive government of Franklin Delano Roosevelt, with the purpose of righting so much injustice, was changing the methods, the previously advocated policy of "THE GREAT GARROTE" Big Stick, with its expansionist policy was changed by that of Good Neighborhood in 1933, "GOOD DEAL" with a policy open to progress. Although the president had inherited the consequences of the great depression, with the help of his wife Eleanor Roosevelt, he was healing the nation, creating new sources of work, partly due to World War II, in which Japanese imperialism precipitated with its surprise attack on the US military base at Pearl Harbor in Hawaii.

At the international conference in Yalta in February 1945, the three leaders discussed the end of the struggle of Joseph Stalin, Winston Churchill and Franklin Delano Roosevelt in World War II, against Germany, Italy and Japan, the latter surrendered unconditionally, after two atomic bombs fell on Hiroshima and Nagasaki, forcing them to sign the end of the war. Roosevelt died before the war ended that same year, after having signed what was called the Atlantic Pact, he was succeeded by his vice president Harry Truman.

Roosevelt and his wife Eleanor, although they had to overcome a very difficult period of government with the Great Depression, the economic recovery and the Second World War, distinguished themselves by cleaning up the neuralgic parts of the nation and pulling it out of chaos.

Geronimo: chief of the Apaches

Crazy horse: chief of the Sioux

THE MONROE DOCTRINE

This is proclaimed in 1823 by James Monroe and his Secretary of State John Quincy Adams. A main motivation was the French intervention in Mexican territory, with the arrival of Emperor Maximilian of Austria, ordered by Napoleon the third. According to some historians, this was presented due to a request from some noble Mexican families of the wealthy classes, dissatisfied with the election as president of Don Benito Juárez, an Indian from the Oaxaca region, an illustrious jurist called: The "Meritorious of the Americas", but since he was not white, they considered him unfit to occupy the first magistracy and they traveled to France to ask the French monarch to appoint someone from the royal family to govern Mexico. France fulfilled their wish by appointing a tall, blond, blue-eyed nobleman of the court, Maximilian of Austria with his wife Charlotte.

The Monroe Doctrine is proclaimed as a message to foreign powers in the American hemisphere, with the premise that they would not tolerate any more interventions, except theirs. Theodore Roosevelt already in the 20th century, December 6, 1904, in his expansionist corollary, denounces the naval blockade of Venezuela by the British-German Empire for the debts contracted and in default of paying them by its president at the time, Cipriano Castro. Without going too far, Washington in 1796, interpreting the thought of Thomas Jefferson, said: "America has a hemisphere to itself, like its own country."

James Polk implored the doctrine during the war with Texas. Bolívar and Santander in the years that were realistic, felt protected from the Spanish empire in Colombia, since it was in the crosshairs of many imperialisms due to its privileged geographical position. Military interventions were frequent and the order of the day. In 1965 the United States flagrantly did it to the

Dominican Republic, while the Russian Brezhnev did it to a defenseless nation like Czechoslovakia.

Burial of massacred Indians

ESTABLISHING A NEW EMPIRE

The United States, from the beginning and when cutting its ties with the British Empire, always wanted to imitate it and stand out as a great power, they faithfully copied the forms, images and concepts of what military power represented, the authoritarian preponderance of what was imperial Rome; even its Hellenic architecture reflected in the great public buildings, its Praetorian Guard, with many-star generals, a great mercantilist economy and its overwhelming expansionism. Perhaps what he has forgotten to keep in mind is that everything has its time and that a large majority of empires have collapsed due to the weight of their excesses.

The only viable formula for not disappearing is not to remain static, to evolve to a more modern, democratic and humanistic society, forgetting the outdated formulas that have only given it difficulties and gratuitous enemies; worrying about not electing warmongering candidates that compromise it internationally, paying attention to internal social problems, cleaning up its economy, monitoring the democratic exercise of the parties and making its industrial power an achievement to grow, enjoy and share.

THE IMPERIALIST STRUGGLES

North America, as a nascent empire, adopted the tasks of its predecessors, but not before having been denounced for their criminal pretensions: a vox populi by heroes such as Simon Bolivar and Jose Marti, the latter said: "I know the dragon, I lived in its in his entrails." Years later, a Mexican dictator like Porfirio Diaz made the expression famous: "Poor Mexico, so far from God and so close to the United States."

Latin America, the Back Yard, which meant for the United States a simple source of resources, has more than paid its submissive rulers or servants and severely punished those who opposed its tutelage, from this generous and lavish pantry began to arrive: coffee, gold, emeralds from Colombia, sugar from Cuba, oil from Venezuela, copper from Chile, tin and silver from Bolivia, fruits from Central America, meat from Argentina, flowers from Ecuador , wood and rubber from Brazil and much more, with the advantage that they are the ones who set the price on the New York Stock Exchange, Wall Street.

A policy to maintain the dependency of these nations was the loans years ago, the debts were backed by the intervention of the marines, each nation in Latin America is indebted and before they finish paying, the contracts are renewed again with leonine interests. Before the end of their term, each new ruler wants to bite the bullet like the previous one and leave the nation more indebted.

On the other hand, the United States has a large market for its excess products: cars, electrical items, Hollywood movies, cigarettes, liquor, chewing gum, opioids, canned goods, brand name items and especially weapons of all kinds and even the most sophisticated with the service and technology to use them. From Mexico they have always taken advantage of cheap labor, their agriculture has depended on their laborers hired for harvest seasons. In the big cities, cleaning, construction and other jobs that, due to their rudeness and danger, the white community rejects; undocumented are accepted to replace them.

But the worst political blunder, flagrantly committed by the State Department in its fear of communism, with the sinister Edgard Hoover at the CIA. and F.B.I. was to promote from the beginning the establishment of disgraceful right-wing military dictatorships, thus coups proliferated in Latin American nations, which received their support and weapons, such as: Castillo Armas in Guatemala, Fulgencio Batista in Cuba, Leónidas Trujillo in the Dominican Republic, Duvalier in Haiti, Anastasio Somoza in Nicaragua, Juan Vicente Gómez and Pérez Jiménez in Venezuela, Noriega in Panama, Rojas Pinilla in Colombia, Odría in Peru, Stroessner in Paraguay, Videla and his board in Argentina and in more recent times Augusto Pinochet in Chile. The gringo intelligence did not care much, that these nations were subjugated, looted and oppressed by these barracks despots and then went out to enjoy the stolen millions. The most important thing was to stop Marxism.

His fear of the statements of Marx and Engels and the diligent work of Lenin, led him to create a school for future despots: Casa de las Américas, in Panama with a super millionaire budget, where an elite of henchmen such as: Ranfis Trujillo, son of the Dominican dictator Rafael Leónidas and his son-in-law Porfirio Rubirosa, Castillo Armas and Anastasio Somoza, also trained by Israeli legionnaires whose soundest thinking could give thirty years in prison. All this financed at the expense of the American people, since these fraudulent practices were carried out with a great curtain of silence, they also had carte blanche to commit crimes and outrages with the Saint Benedict that they were defending democracy. In the same way, the church in colonial times committed so many barbarities and injustices with the so-called Holy Inquisition, under the pretext of preserving Christian virtues.

Courtesy Amon Carter Museum, Fort W

Native Americans and buffalo were heavily fought

THE DARK EFFECTS OF McCARTISM

The unfounded fear that the ideas of Marx and Engels would spread politically in America caused a witch hunt to appear, in high places they saw communists stationed everywhere, ready to strike. In 1947 in New York, some centers of the film industry considered it infected by the Marxist virus, which caused a committee investigating Anti-American activities, invoking the Fifth Amendment, to draw up a blacklist of red sympathizers, to prosecute and imprison them those who refused to testify.

Joseph McCarthy, senator for the state of Wisconsin during the short time he participated in the legislative field, was notorious in government as a political bigot, seeking prominence and becoming important for the battles he led as leader of the Republican ultra-right, fomenting a: fight without quarter with their denunciations and persecutions against a hundred notables, scientists, actors and intellectuals, of being influenced by communists, in the most critical periods of the Cold War. Period that historian Doris Kearns describes in her works as one of the most destructive in national political history. The senator claimed to have in his possession the list of compromised officials within the State Department and creating a Committee for the Investigation of Anti-American Activities. It all ended in 1954, when the unfounded accusations of the senator were proven by not finding the evidence of these accusations against film personalities such as: Charles Chaplin and Humphrey Bogard and high-ranking military members such as Joseph Wellch, who managed to disrupt with facts that they were all falsehoods. In the end, there was no attack, nor did they find the communist spies, nor their weapons, which they believed existed, nor contacts with Moscow. It was all a very well-staged hoax to scare the highest political circles.

The then director of the CIA. Edgard Hoover, had a lot to do with a series of investigations that had no foundation or credibility, he abused the enormous power he controlled, within these institutions with secret Gestapo-type operations, with a wide network of connections by around the world, in which several presidents could not stop their feverish and bellicose mind, among them the Kennedy brothers, Nixon and Johnson.

Edgard Hoover was another dark page of the MacChartist Era, many of his biographies mention him as an unscrupulous man, who managed to obtain a lot of compromising information with the enormous budget available to politicians who feared him. This obscure official had to do with illegal activities, such as providing funds and hiring characters to carry out the WATERGATE operation, for which Nixon was forced to resign as president, as well as other irregularities in the Reagan administration, in the case: Iran contras.

Before leaving office, Hoover managed to destroy much evidence that compromised him for his sexual deviations and abuse of power, he was a man as feared as James Hoffa, gangster type, director of unions and transport unions.

It is not uncommon for the day to come when someone explores Hoover's compromising story in the death of Jorge Eliecer Gaitán, in Colombia, 1948 when the top officials of both the Liberal and Conservative parties petitioned the State Department to free them from the threat posed by the populist leader of the revolutionary left; It will be necessary for the CIA and the FBI to allow the archives of such sinister days to be read, but I do not see this possible until a hundred years have passed, by then they will no longer be interested in knowing the truth, and how committed the Colombian ruling classes were from then, in what was called: the Bogotazo, taking advantage of the meeting of the Pan American Union, with the presence of Mr. Marshall and the creation of the O.E.A.

Immediately, I kicked off my shoe and started to take off my shoelaces. The van did have an alarm as it was used mainly for transporting a variety of artist's work to a variety of shows. Since that was part of my mom's job as an art director.

But it was no problem as I had disabled the alarm using an after market switch I had discovered on the vehicle while using it for the last two to three days. All I had to do was press and hold the button for five seconds as the red light on the dash blinked off. I had done so after parking the van in the garage.

The hard part was over.

I looped my shoelace into a slipknot and shimmied it behind the rubber lining of the door. Then I lowered the string and aligned the loop over the nub of the locking mechanism. I pulled the loop taunt and lifted the string.

The nub came up easy.

The door was unlocked.

I silently thanked Trey for teaching me the trick before opening the driver's side door.

Once inside, I hopped in the back of the van.

It was dark.

Darker than it had been in the garage which had been semi-dark because of the light shining through the window.

I would have used the electronic council on the door to unlock the back but I had no key to turn the ignition on. And I had no time to hotwire the van for that reason alone. So, I waited ten seconds for my eyes to adjust to the dark.

It worked, but barley.

The light coming in through the front of the van seemed to increase with intensity as if the sun outside had become free of clouds.

I took the opportunity.

I stepped around the duffle bags and grabbed the handle.

The doors opened with ease.

I stepped out of the van and tried to think for a moment.

I had no real plan other than to not get caught. Which was of course no plan at all. Where was I going to hide the money?

I looked around the garage.

It seemed hopeless.

I was thinking about throwing the duffle bags out the window, one by one, and then trying to fit my big ass through. Then hiking to a spot in the woods to bury the money. It seemed like an okay plan but it would take too much time to dig a hole.

I was also tired.

Instead, I opted for plan b.

Stuffing the money in the storage attic of the garage.

As I grabbed the first duffle bag and climbed the ladder, which was embedded into the wall and looked like empty shelving, I thought to myself, that it was probably one of the better spots on the property to hide shit.

I lifted the trapdoor slowly, careful not to make any noise, and climbed the rest of the way up.

It was darkest up here; there were no windows. Which made it appear as if there was no attic, when comparing and contrasting the outside from the inside, at least. Everything was uniform.

I didn't bother turning on the light; the switch was a string dangling in the middle of the room somewhere, and would require me to grope through the darkness to find it. Instead I piled the bags one by one, against the wall, behind the trap door. I did so, in such a way, that anyone looking for the money would have to come into the room and find the light switch first to find the money.

In other words, they simply couldn't reach behind the trap door to feel for the duffle bags. Which would have been impossible anyways given the position of the ladder.

When I was finished, I crawled on my hands and knees, as the height and slant of the ceiling was severe and steep. My face found the string before my hands did. I reached up and unscrewed the bulb.

I put it in my pocket and crawled back across the floor to the trap door.

I'd have to fix it better later. Maybe find something to drape or put in front of the duffle bags. But for right now all I could think about was getting back to my room without getting caught and going to sleep for a few hours.

My bed was calling me.

I went down the ladder that looked like shelving and closed the trap door behind me. Then I went over to the van and opened the driver's side door. I reset the car alarm by holding in the switch for five seconds.

Once the red light on the dash was blinking I locked and shut the door.

I climbed the steps to the kitchen and carefully opened the door a crack. I peeked inside to discover Annie distracting officer Miley. She stood before him as he sat on the sofa facing the other way.

THE COLD WAR

This secret and underground policy has existed in almost all times, it was not only the United States and the Soviet Union that were responsible, but also the bloc of nations that were not under the influence of Moscow, considered to be on the Western side: France, Germany, Switzerland, England, Belgium and others. The Cold War practically began after the Second World War, due to political ideologies.

The Soviet Union formed a group of surrounding and allied nations militarily and economically governed with Marxist-Leninist doctrines in 1922, Ukraine, Belarus, Armenia, Azerbaijan and Georgia. Sometime later a small group of neighboring countries joined. In the same way with the eastern sector of Germany, in which frequent escapes of deserters began to appear towards the western sector controlled by the allies: the United States and others. The communists erected a large wall, complete with watchtowers to discourage defection, but defection nonetheless continued for a long time with frequent skirmishes.

The struggle for supremacy, after the allies defeated fascist ideas in Europe: Mussolini in Italy, Hitler in Germany, only Falangism remained in Spain, with Francisco Franco with his authoritarian, right-wing Falangist doctrine, supported by the Catholic Church, who in his early stages joined Hitler and Mussolini.

The world was struggling at a crossroads: What would be, in philosophical and political terms, the ideas that would dominate the world, after the theses of THE SUPER MAN, supported by Federico Nietzsche in his work: Thus Spake Zarathustra, were defeated? And that fed the sick mind of Adolf Hitler with his book: MY STRUGGLE.

The other possibility that was noted as a great threat to dominate the world was COMMUNISM. Lenin and Stalin had managed, with the help of the Bolshevik army, to defeat the monarchical government of Tsar Nicolas II Romanoff and impose another authoritarian government in their struggle for power, which sacrificed entire generations in extermination camps in Siberia Gulags, and ordered the murder of Trozky in Mexico, before normalizing the situation.

Karl Marx never managed to see his political work done, he died before Lenin and Stalin implanted it in Russia, at a cost of 30 million victims.

For the moment after the end of the Second World War, the philosophy that emerged was that of defeatism and despair: Jean Paul Sartre's Existentialism, because on the horizon there was no glimpse of hope, but omens of a third conflict with the nightmare of a radioactive fungus.

Within existentialism, there are many trends including the one advocated by Albert Camus, another Nobel Prize winner with his Christian existentialism, but this goes back years to the tasks of the Danish philosopher: Soren Kierkegaard, considering human existence in an unfathomable universe, also condemning the principles of other fellow philosophers, such as Hegel's. Another great teacher and author were the German Martin Heidegger, who opposed accepting the term existentialist to cover these philosophical thoughts, including the Hegelian dialectic. Sartre always maintained that he was the only existentialist.

In the political part, worldwide espionage became very notorious, the critical part was the development of nuclear weapons, it was also the time of the Jewish spies Julius and Ethel Rosenberg, arrested in 1950 and sentenced to death for delivering secrets to Russia of atomic weapons and which had a great impact worldwide. Judge Irving Kaufman charged the couple with Altering the Course of History and they were convicted of treason and died in the electric chair on the night of June 19, 1953. While the trial lasted there was a huge demand from all over the celebrity world. Requesting the commutation of the death sentence.

Then there was the shooting down of a very sophisticated American U2 spy plane over Russian territory commanded by Gary Power on May 1, 1960, with highly compromising confiscated photographic material that Nikita Khrushchev reported to the United Nations. Power was saved from death by being traded for another Soviet spy.

During the years of the Cold War, both the military such as: Douglas MacArthur and D. Eisenhower, had much preponderance in the idea of continuing the war actions, Truman had to stop the fiery military man of the exotic pipes, who intended to expand the bombings in China, beyond the Yalu River. As for Eisenhower, in 1955 he left the Vietnam War started, when his presidential term ended, he left the invasion of Cuba armed to John Kennedy so that he would initiate it with the full conviction that it would have a guaranteed success.

There were very critical moments and we were on the verge of a third world war, but the reciprocal fear of a conflict without winners, but rather both losers, with the destructive power of the hydrogen bomb and the proliferation of radioactive fungi, discouraged the two powers.

It is important to give credit to the memory of Nikita Khrushchev, who practically gave up the ground to dismantle the nuclear bases already installed in Cuba, speak of peaceful coexistence and unmask the legend of Stalin as the true executioner of the Russian people, it was the era of the great famines and persecutions, he sacrificed many of his compatriots, whom I consider political enemies in his eagerness to handle power alone. The so-called cold war practically ended in the last decades, with the abandonment of the primers of Marx, Lenin and Mao by Russia and China of catechizing the globe with a communist policy and embracing free enterprise and the search for new markets for their products, regardless of the so-called struggle of the proletariat. The capitalism against which Marx and Engels fought in their time, was no longer even a shadow, there have been many important changes.

Although there was not officially a condemnation of Marxism and the doctrines of Lenin, these were defeated by a new opening that was called: Glasnov, originated by the Soviet leader Mikhail Gorbachev in a clear opposition to the tyranny of the party, orthodox and authoritarian, embers of the system implemented by Lósif Stalin, which had lost a lot of prestige and had slowed down the economy in 1990.

The violence and cruelty of an unpopular war.

Dramatic photos of the excesses in Vietnam by the army

THE AMERICAN DREAM

"I dreamed that I saw myself in a more flattering state"

Calderón de La Barca, Life is a dream.

American society can be considered as an idealistic dream, worth imitating and whose model is the perfect way of living on the globe. This is the society for which an immigrant is worth leaving his native land, separating from his loved ones to start a new way of life and achieve the objectives that many consider as the maximum expression achieved in terms of success and individual freedoms.

What has been the reason why the Republican administration of Donald Trump saw the need to build an impregnable wall of enormous proportions on the southern border with Mexico, to contain the human waves of Central Americans fleeing corruption and misgovernment, in search for that American dream, proclaimed through all the media as the richest society in the world? Years ago, Kennedy led to the collapse of the Berlin Wall because he considered it inhumane, he never thought that a republican government would build in his country, a higher and more extensive one, we refer to the one that Donald Trump left unfinished, by not achieving his re-election and for which he intended force Mexico to pay for it.

America First (First America), an old slogan that Trump enthroned again as if it were his, where in a few days you can become a millionaire man, enjoy infinite comforts, buy a new car and a house, live fully in a society democracy that offers you a myriad of opportunities that yours and other countries deny you. Is it true what you have seen in movies, television and other media, corroborated by the remittances of dollars from various countrymen and the promises of power emigrate the whole family to give them the best education in a short time?

Many of these opportunities are true, but not for everyone, only a small minority manages to achieve them. It is obvious that if you belong to the Aryan race, speak English without an accent, have a well-paid profession, already have a formal education with academic degrees and are well connected politically, the doors can be easily opened, in this case "the dream American" is doable. Such is the case of a German immigrant of Jewish origin, born in Furth in 1923, whose family managed to emigrate in his adolescence, but of which 14 died, in concentration camps, in 1938 he first arrived in London, without speaking English, but he learned it quickly, of course he always had a twangy accent, it was easier to understand a Turko throwing up, despite that he was accepted at Harvard, he wore thick glasses, called bottle bottoms and had stinky breath who shooed away even flies, but became a professor years later at the same university and since he liked politics, in North America he managed to be an adviser to Presidents such as: Kennedy and Johnson and continued to climb positions until he was appointed Secretary of State for Nixon , of whom he said was inept and did not measure up to be president, taking advantage of the ignorance in geography and history of these Presidents, not to go any further, in a short time he will be one hundred years old, his name is Henry Kissinger.

Henry Kissinger for his recommendations to exterminate several Asian nations, Nixon and Johnson as an official of their administrations and plan the overthrow and assassination of a government like the Chilean Salvador Allende, advisor to the Condor program in Panama, Casa de Las Americas, He is known in the political scene as: The Exterminating Angel.

Now Magazine (England): Kissinger Memoirs

Kissinger was called: the exterminating angel for all the excesses he committed during his hegemony in the State Department.

The arms balance with powerful nuclear rockets has prolonged the peace.

PARADISE LOST

Many migrants who arrived in the United States late to enjoy it, were convinced that almost everything was not a dream but a nightmare, although given the reality in which many nations from which they emigrate live, there may be a paradise recovered, if they are leaving countries subjugated by dictatorships of the right and left, political persecution, famine, lack of opportunities, corruption, etc.

The wait for undocumented immigrants to fix papers is taking many years and the costs of lawyers are stratospheric, the competition to find work becomes more difficult every day for those who do not speak the English language and do not have a defined profession or university studies. It is very possible that you will have to return to your country of origin to legalize your papers and wait for an appointment at the American Consulate. Raids and deportations are becoming more and more frequent; It is important to be forewarned and do not forget these recommendations if you do not have legal papers:

• Avoid getting drunk in public places and being arrested.

• Carry weapons of any kind,

• Driving without a license.

• Participate in street fights.

• Walking drugged through public places.

• Buy fake IDs.

• Not respect traffic laws or as a pedestrian.

• Avoid family fights or scandals.

• Keep a phone list of attorneys or bondsmen.

• Above all, do not sign any document authorizing your deportation.

But all is not lost, paradise exists if you want to call it that, face living reality according to the law, there are still some opportunities. Canada is to the north and they are offering many possibilities to immigrants as well.

THE OTHER SOVIET PARADISE

Although Russia, after having deposed the iron dictatorship of Tsar Nicholas II Romanoff in 1917 with the Bolshevik army, it was considered that the great nightmare of the authoritarian and hegemonic governments would end for the people, which would give them a break after the First World War, which at end would have a government that would respect human beings for what they are, a civil democratic society with its opposition parties and constructive, no more monarchs, or elitist governments; but what came later was worse than what was left behind, since a bloody and fierce struggle for power was established, in which the following emerged as political protagonists: Peter Illich Lenin, Joseph Stalin and others.

They dissolved the first Governing Board controlled by Alexander Kerensky, but another fight ensued and Lenin with secret police proclaimed himself supreme chief, but was about to be assassinated in 1918 by another group called: The Red Terror. Lenin was the one who gave the orders to assassinate the entire Tsarist family, and ruled Russia for a period that lasted six years until his death in 1924 from a stroke.

Karl Marx, founder of the Communist party with Engels, in 1847 died in 1883 before seeing his dream come true with his work: "Capital, Das Kapital the Communist Manifesto", theories and programs for a Proletarian Society, which at that time were considered just and an alternative to a dehumanized materialist capitalism like the one that reigned in the imperialist powers. But if Marx had lived, he would have been disappointed to have witnessed so many crimes to impose his theories. The remedy was worse than the disease.

The true positive result of the fruits of Marxism could not be appreciated, they were spoiled by the struggle for power of some leaders for wanting to perpetuate themselves.Something similar happened with the teachings of Jesus of Nazareth, who preached peace, love, brotherhood and his followers later did the opposite of his statements.

Returning to the course of history, after Lenin, Stalin inherited power and installed another terror regime in which many millions succumbed to those he considered his enemies, in forced labor camps in Siberia: Gulag. Trotsky, his companion who managed to flee to Mexico, lived for a while in the house of muralist Diego Rivera and Frida Kahlo, his comrades as well, until he was caught up by a party henchman, Ramon Mercader of Puerto Rican origin, who served as his secretary for a while he was preparing how to assassinate him with an axe, on Stalin's personal orders, but during his dictatorship there were many comrades from the party's elite that he took it upon himself to liquidate, fearful of having to share power, corroborated by another Party leader social worker, who later denounced the crimes of Stalin, his name was Nikita Khrushchev, the party began to be called the Communist Party on October 25, 1918.

The Russian people experienced terrible suffering for many decades, not only with the tyranny of the Tsar, then with the Napoleonic Invasion, then followed two world wars and then the criminal struggle for power of their comrade leaders, with famines, devastation, forced labor, imprisonments and collective massacres.

What came later was the formation of what was called the Union of Soviet Socialist Republics (Soviet Paradise), a totalitarian regime with a single political party that is the proletariat, ended in 1991, with Glasnov, and Perestroika during the government of Boris Yeltsin and Mikhail Gorbachev.

What almost does not appear, are the requests of foreign citizens wanting to integrate into the Soviet Society as resident citizens to enjoy the advantages of their paradise, the Russian consulates do not have the siege of applicants, which the Americans have. But don't forget, both systems have their shells and demons.

The Comrades in the last century were very active.The Communist Party had its moment, but it did not prosper in membership.

THE SYMBOLS OF THE UNION

When some notable patriots considered the need to find grandiose symbols for the American Union that would encourage nationalist love, and felt proud every time they saw these emblems, as happened in Germany when the Nazis contemplated a multitude of flags with the swastika, the Jews with the star of David, the communists the oz and the hammer and the Spanish Francoists the symbol of the phalanx.

The Americans were looking for a complement to their already glorious flag of "the stars and stripes", initially California with its perhaps separatist idea when it was still part of Mexico, found in the bear the corpulent power and its fearsome claws to discourage any California Republic intervention, sometime later the bear was given a forest ranger uniform, but less aggressive. The Russians have also adopted this animal as a symbol of power and aggressiveness.

Another notable American whose name I do not remember, perhaps, Mr. Neras suggested the wild figure of the turkey of the forests (a good pisco), of great majesty when its plumage dwindles, but more than all because in colonial times, in the English community of Massachusetts a handful of native Indians, in a harsh winter saved the life and from a great famine to a group of Quaker parishioners, already dying, with pumpkins, vegetables, fruits, ducks and turkeys.

Since then, the turkey has become the favorite meat to celebrate: Thanksgiving: Thanksgiving, an important date in the national calendar. But the turkey did not have claws, nor is it an aggressive animal, rather tamable, that is why it was rejected. It is said that a soldier proposed the bald eagle for its aggressiveness, airy and combative, and in the end, the warmongering proposal won.

Since then, the veneration of the bald eagle began for its majestic bearing, considered the king of the forests, mountains and American plains, but above all for its combativeness and power of its claws, emblem of war.

The native inhabitants of the American steppes used their colorful plumage to adorn their heads and clothing; their secular dances are very colorful and imitate the movements of the bird in the mating period, due to its splendid plumage, they almost end with them. Now it is the most protected bird in the union.

Colombia adopted the condor of the Andes, with a majestic crest and white neck for its tricolor shield that surpasses the eagle in volume and in the extension of its wings, in exchange for a nation that has an entire continent to fly, the Andes Mountain range.

The flag of the American Union is of great beauty, its stars represent the 50 states and the bars the 13 original states, it is hoisted in public and private buildings, particularly on holidays, but there is no respect for it, because of its many colors. People use it in all forms, especially women in sports shirts, bikinis, towels, cushions, furniture linings, table cloths, market bags, doll dresses and in everything that the imagination suggests. The existing anti-Americanism in many parts, buys it to burn it in special events.

Other symbols that stand out for the country are: Uncle Sam, the classic American tall, blond with a top hat and striped dress, used in media cartoons. The wild buffalo of great beauty due to its ferocity and corpulence in danger of extinction, the wolf of the woods and the great Liberty Bell of Philadelphia, the Liberty Bell used to rally patriots during the War of Independence.

Of all the patriotic and inspiring symbols of the national soul, the statue of liberty of great beauty stands out, anchored in Manhattan Bay, on Ellis Island, through which millions of immigrants entered, also a symbol of justice and generous protection, the statue it was a gift from France to the United States as an act of brotherhood and solidarity.

The statue is also the favorite Lai Motiv of critics, cartoonists and media humorists such as Scapegoat, to charge the country with all its mistakes, outrages and ridicule its behavior before the world.

In the defensive plane of the warlike fantasy for America they also show their faces: Superman, the journalist Clark Kent who at the time of action, at the cry of Shazam is invincible, Tarzan of the Apes is in charge of protecting the forests and their fauna , Dick Tracy is in charge of justice in the high courts and is an investigator of underworld crime, Batman and Robin (gay couple), fight crime in a fast car through big cities, Wonder Woman is another vigilante who unforgiving of street crime, Spider-Man prowls high-rise buildings looking for action. As a pioneer of space fantasy in 1933, Flash Gordon traveled to the planet Mongo to save the earth from the tyrant Ming with the scientist Dr. Zarcof.

Although it seems simple nonsense, these characters have helped create a montage of power and supremacy of the American union, some characters like Superman and Batman, many people see them as real and part of their fighting force, especially children. The characters are continuously recreated to animate parties and national celebrations in the same way in the comics and the toy store there are many imitations taken from the movies and TV.

The Turkey **The Bald Eagle**

The two most important birds, emblems of the American national soul.

The most important symbols of the American union

Uncle Sam

The Bell of Philadelphia

The Stars and Stripes Flag

Statue of Liberty

POLITICAL PARTIES IN THE USA HOW IS THE BUREAUCRATIC CAKE DIVIDED?

Two main political groups govern the territory of the American Union, through the result of presidential elections, every four years and in order to vote, citizenship is required by birth or through legal immigration status obtained in a very solemn ceremony, in which it is sworn loyalty and defend the nation when she demands it.

The parties are Democratic and Republican. There are other minor parties such as El Libertario and others with other names, but in practice it is the first two mentioned that have been in operation since the end of the civil war. The Republican Party was founded in 1854 by those who opposed the extension of slavery in the new territories and led by Abraham Lincoln, in 1880 they called themselves: The Grand Old Party with the acronym GOP.

At the beginning of the party organization was called: Whig Party the most important of them for the election of 1832, was the Democratic Party and Andrew Jackson was elected for two terms. In 1840 a party with the name of "The Know Nothing" (We know nothing), which later adopted the name of Republican, a time of great uncertainty and the problem of slavery had not been completely cleared up. The Republicans were the Northerners, while the Democrats were down south as cotton farmers: Cotton Whigs. After having adopted a series of amendments that were made in order to achieve the reorganization of the government in each state, and that took a long time to implement.

The elephant was chosen by the Republican Party to represent its pachydermia pretensions and overwhelming movements, a symbol of power and strength, the Democrats, for their part, found in a donkey, the model to represent their stubbornness and patience.

Its conventions are very noisy, carnival-like, with plenty of confetti, balloons, flags and very strident music that lasts for several days, where the candidates and vice-presidential candidates are chosen: The Ticket.

As far as the colors are concerned, it seems that there was a confusion from the beginning, it is not known why, but the Republicans, who are so conservative and ultra-right wing, have the color red; Worldwide adopted by the communists in Russia and China adorned by Oz and The Hammer, it has also been used by Liberals and left-wing parties such as in Colombia and Spain, where the Socialist Party has used the color red since 1977.

Conservatives in other parts of the world, especially elites and royalty who speak of blue blood, the same as Aryans with eye color. Emperors and Kings have always had a preference for blue. The American flag has 50 white stars on a blue background and its bars are red.

The Democratic Party has distinguished itself for being more open and vigilant, the favorite of minorities, tolerant and ready for reforms, progress and necessary changes. On the other hand, the Republican Party brings together the plutocracy, intolerance, racism, the ultra-conservative and warmongering elites; It is no more than consulting history to see how its characters have behaved: Theodore Roosevelt, authoritarian and expansionist, Warren Harding, tolerated a lot of corruption, George Wallace, a racist and intolerant, was a segregationist and it is not known why he was enrolled with the Democrats, Ronald Reagan, a warmonger , and little friend of minorities, corrupt and warmongering Richard Nixon, was forced to resign for inappropriate and shameful behavior, as was Spiro Agnew, Vice President. Bush father and son, both Republicans, were also characterized by starting wars and friends of engaging in conflicts in oil nations.

And in more recent years Donald Trump, racist, undiplomatic, aggressive, warmonger, investigated for trying to evade taxes, along with his family, at the last minute promoted riots in the Capitol, in which there were several deaths, for not wanting to accept his defeat, Barry Goldwater, another Republican candidate also let his devilish racism feel.

It is important to clarify as part of the political history of this country, that it had a socialist workers' party since 1919, to which Lenin invited some more active members of the left to better join the so-called: Communist International, which was being formed in many countries and which was joined by important figures of anarchism, given that in the early stages of the formation of capitalism, it was slave-owning and maintained an iniquitous and exploitative system of exploiting workers with 14-hour work days, many foremen used the whip, low wages and there was a great mortality in children and women were the results.

For a long time, the communist party was active in America and had its conventions like the other two Democratic and Republican parties, it reached 25,000 followers, however it could not prosper, and most of its leaders were imprisoned and constantly investigated. The crimes of Stalin and the frequent purges of the party in Russia discouraged many, other factors, the assassination of Trozky, totalitarianism, the Siberian Gulaps camps, were definitive in ending sympathy for the party of the proletariat. Gus Hall in America, was always its eternal leader and candidate for the presidency, Angela Davis, as an activist of the Black Panthers, also figured as a leader.

Abraham Lincoln is the only republican who appears in history as the most egregious figure, who achieved the Freedom of the slaves. He was assassinated by an anarchist, theater actor. It is important to recognize that not all Democratic presidents have been an example of virtues, several of them have also been investigated, but in the balance of history, the Democrats have better behaviors in their favor.

In the electoral process of the American Union, a shameful custom has been fostered that lends itself so that the current president, holding power, allows him to campaign for re-election using all his privileges, vehicles, plans, helicopters for transportation and even money from the been in your favour. This should be considered unethical and unethical. The president had to request a permit from Congress for a temporary withdrawal from the government, while he campaigns and does not use time, salaries, or services in his favor, the vice president had to take command as head until the end of the period of elections, if the president decides to seek a second term.

It is important to note that capitalist democracy, in which several political parties participate, does not have that proselytizing character that communism has, of a single totalitarian party and in most cases controlled by an authoritarian military clique with the desire to perpetuate itself in the world. Dog. There are no political indoctrination primers.

What is very unfortunate is the ignorance of many candidates, a large majority do not know geography or history; It is said that when a Colombian ambassador presented President Ronald Reagan, the country's highest distinction, in a ceremonial act at the embassy in Washington, the president replied: "I feel very grateful to my Bolivian friends for this present." Nixon and Johnson did not know where some of the nations they had ordered to bomb were located, with the conflict in Vietnam.

Before voting, the American people should learn more about the candidates, not vote for men, but for programs so that the nightmare they had with Donald Trump does not happen to them and always remember the advice left to us by the great philosopher George Orwell:

FORBIDDEN TO FORGET:

A town that chooses corrupt, impostors, thieves and traitors

He is not a victim; he is an accomplice.

Abraham Lincoln

The great apostle of freedom

US FOREIGN POLICY
How to win enemies and make yourself hated?

If you sow tares, do not expect to reap wheat.

D.H.

On several occasions, the North American foreign policy of different Republican and Democratic administrations have made great mistakes, which have not only cost the public treasury millions and millions, but their prestige has been on the ground, the lack of tolerance and the role of police of the world that they have wanted to appropriate, waging war against nations that have never attacked them, simply to maintain the inappropriate warmongering spirit, unfortunately to follow the advice of officials or soldiers who have passed through the White House with criminal intentions, compromising the nation and endangering the lives of many beings. It seems that White House intelligence read Dale Carnegie's book: How to Win Friends, but put it into practice backwards or in the opposite direction.

In their idea of becoming a great empire like Great Britain, the Soviet Union or Continental China, there were many incursions that they made in Latin America in their expansionist desire, causing so many deaths and finally sponsoring military dictatorships of satraps and tyrants, that apart from looting their economies, they carried out frequent massacres and kept the towns in obscurantism and secular backwardness. Such is the abominable case of: Rafael Leónidas Trujillo in the Dominican Republic, Anastasio Somoza in Nicaragua, Duvalier in Haiti, Pérez Jiménez in Venezuela, Odría in Peru, Stroessner in Paraguay, Castillo Armas in Guatemala, Fulgencio Batista in Cuba, Noriega in Panama, Augusto Pinochet in Chile and the shadowy Military Junta in Argentina led by Videla.

Many of these tyrants remained in power for several decades, with military protection and economic aid from the State Department, only in exchange for opening the door to companies that plundered their economies, to banks that granted loans, and kept the nation in debt. But mainly to defeat any progressive idea or that spoke of socialism. This unintelligent and corrupt blindness of sponsoring criminal sergeants with continuityist ideas had its fruits, they pushed Cuba to communism and engendered a hatred of the United States that they have not yet been able to erase.

The proof of the anti-Americanism that they propitiated themselves with their mistaken policy was received in Nixon's shaved face, spit and burned American flags in various parts of Latin America, when he was doing his political campaign, on a trip through Latin America. In the same way, Nelson Rockefeller was able to convince himself that things were not going very well in the backyard due to the wrong management of the White House.

When imperialist France lost the war of liberation against Vietnam, after a conflict of so many years of attrition and loss of life, in an unintelligent move the brains of the pentagon asked Kennedy to fill the void. The United States did not learn the lesson and soon ran to take the place of France, due to the advice of military men like Eisenhower, Douglas MacArthur that such strategic places in Indochina could not be abandoned, and they also thought that by entering the North American war power, Ho Chi Ming would be ready to give up and not continue the fight, because they were wrong and fell into the trap, misguided by the foster brothers and Allan Dulles and other White House colonels.

John Kennedy had been very successful in amorous but not military conquests, inexperienced, ill-advised and unwise, his first failure was the Bay of Pigs with all the aggravations, many of the legionnaires after the defeat were shot and others pardoned in exchange for products pharmacists. World War III almost broke out.

The Mafias charged the Kennedys for not having continued the war in Cuba, since they lost their preponderance in the Caribbean. Jack and Robert were murdered. The Conference of Nations meeting in Genoa proposed to divide Vietnam into two parts, North and South as was done in Korea along the 17th Parallel. Something similar happened with the Irish territory, North and South. Divide to rule: Machiavellian thesis.

After the Korean War, Vietnam was divided: the communist north was fighting for its total integration, but the south had other pretensions. A group of soldiers from South Vietnam, dazzled by the dollars, some copies of Playboy magazine and the promise of taking them to Disneyland, agreed to destabilize the Catholic government of the Dinh Diem brothers, assassinating them and with the approval of the then president. John Kennedy, also another Catholic, by not lending himself to continue the fight against North Vietnam by staging a coup. By 1962 there were 9,000 American soldiers on the warpath.

What accelerated the conflict was the destruction of two destroyers in the Gulf of Tonkin in 1963; it is rumored that the Americans themselves did it, to have the reason for the massive bombing they carried out on North Vietnam.

Then the worst came, the American soldiers fought almost drugged with marijuana, there was a lot of liquor, and beer to keep the boys doped and happy in such an unjust, unpopular war with no chance of winning it.

Chemicals like Orange, Napalm in large doses, inhumane massacres like the one in Mylai, millions of tons of bombs over the North, Laos and Cambodia with bombardments from saturation over farm fields to nations that had never attacked them with words. In 1969, half a million soldiers were already in combat. In America, the demonstrations for peace were neglected, alleging that everything was about to end.

It took seven long years of attrition and death for them to understand that not everything can be won with weapons. Lindon Johnson had prepared a plan to end the war, but Kissinger and Nixon beat him to it when they were campaigning for president, saying that their plan was better and that the end of the war with them was just around the corner, but everything turned out to be lies and they prolonged it for seven more years.

This was the most unpopular war that the United States has ever had, which caused so many lives and so many billions of dollars, Johnson's resignation to a second term, the rise of the Hippie Society, opposed to the continuation of the conflict, a worldwide outcry because it will end and the soldiers will return. Many did return but in aluminum mortuary boxes wrapped in the stars and stripes flag.

Soldiers like McNamara told the people: We were wrong, sorry with many exquiusmis before resigning, Wesmoreland said the same thing. General Alexander Haig made so many mistakes that there are thousands of victims of his policies in the territories in conflict, even Reagan was stunned by the coldness with which he recognized his faults.

Nixon refused to accept that they had lost the war as France lost it, the spoke of honor, after Watergate, and so many dead soldiers making the V for victory with their fingers. His departure was shameful and muddied his Republican party, before leaving. I forgive several criminals, for being his friends, among them: Calley and Hoffa. Even his own pardon was requested from his Vice President Ford.

North America had to accept later, a million Vietnamese migrants with their families, who today live as veterans, from their most loyal servants. It would be interesting to imagine the millions of dollars spent on such an inhumane contest, spent on education, food and public services, for your own nation.

We must also consider the crime against Human Rights, respect for the dignity of each being: the elderly, women and children who died in the conflict; It has not yet been forgotten, the moving photographs of the Mylai Massacre, a genocide without justification; the perpetrators of the crime received nothing but simple reprimands and calls for attention. Calley that a court sentenced to twenty years, Nixon pardoned him. After being found guilty in the case of robbing Democratic facilities, Nixon had to resign, but was pardoned by his Vice President G. Ford.

Trump recently pardoned many of his friends, who had prison sentences for serious crimes that is how justice works in America, when it comes to the elites.

The same has been the cover-up of the treatment of detainees in the Guantánamo prison, in Cuban territory, rented by Batista, practically in perpetuity from the United States, where there are Al Qaeda terrorists who have been tortured, with supporting photographs, published by the media, the government responds with another: Sorry.

Now after so many years, unified Vietnam is another country, nobody talks about politics, without corrupt military, with a lot of tourism and exporting many products to the world.

North America not only fought many countries with the excuse of communism, now later with the excuse of terrorism, to justify punitive incursions, such is the case of Iraq that was accused of having a large aggressive armament, President Bush called for an immediate occupation under this pretext and Hussein was overthrown and after a great destruction of Iraq and the death of several thousand inhabitants, including its Leader, Spiritual Imam Hussein, confessed: "We were wrong again, there were no such weapons".

The real reason was oil prices, after so many years Iraq is still adrift, unable to restore order. Another nation has been Libya, this time it was France that destabilized it and overthrew the ruler Omar Khadaffi, and in which the United States also collaborated. Afghanistan was next on the list with operation: Enduring Freedom, considering that the center of the terrorist insurgency was there and the batteries focused on it, because it was on the side of nations such as India and Pakistan.

For several years, Russia had it besieged, it was the time that the United States helped Osama Bin Laden with weapons, when Russia left the conflict, the United States maintained an occupation also for several years until it decided to abandon it, without caring about the deaths in the conflict, and then the Taliban took full control.

Iran, ancient Persia, has been in the sights of all the powers, for its oil wealth, the United States had it on its side, while it had the corrupt government of the Shah, Mahammad Reza Pahlavi, Supreme Emperor, who squandered huge sums of money on an ostentatious life, with great parties and luxuries, was the time of Kissinger who was not lacking in any dinner with caviar and champagne, while the Iranian people suffered from hunger and misery. In the end he was overthrown by Ayathola Komeni, a fundamentalist religious leader in 1979. The Shah had to flee and by then not even North America accepted him as an exile, he was his great friend but it was uncomfortable to have him, like other dictators Batista and Pinochet in his time, they had to find other places to spend their last days.This is how he usually pays his most servile servants.

Western powers are still very vigilant of Iran, how to destabilize it, but since it is now a nuclear power and continues to seek its uranium enrichment, now they speak better of negotiations.

Donald Trump, in his last year in office, ordered a secret punitive raid against an important Iranian military leader: Gasen Soliman, killing him while visiting Baghdad.

Obama during his government ordered an incursion against Osama Bin Laden, of course he had been accused of having prepared the terrorist operation of the twin towers, the pentagon and other official entities and of having caused so many deaths, especially in New York and Washington. In this case there was a justification, but not in the case of the Military in Iran.

With all the power of this nation, with such noble traditions of the first constitutional heroes, with all the vast and immense geography and with all that its controversial behavior has meant, it is inexplicable that in recent times it has had such mediocre leaders, incapable, traitors of their constitution, ill-intentioned and inferior to their historical moment.

Richard Nixon in all defeats considered himself a victor.

Nixon during his political campaign played the role of guide with Khrushchev.

THE GREAT SINS AGAINST THE ENVIRONMENT

Although a large majority is aware that we are progressively committing suicide, with all the sins we commit against planet earth, the house we inhabit, there are a large number of corporations, factories, companies and entities that transgress by poisoning the environment with official licenses, without caring about the great damage they are committing even against themselves, their families and their own interests, contaminating all spaces with the exploitation of fossils.

Although the United States is making great efforts to improve the environmental problem, with great promises for when the promised deadlines are met, the deterioration will be very great and irreversible, since the summer heat is extreme, in the same way the winters are like never before we had them.

As the host country of the United Nations and signatories of environmental protection, it is unacceptable that we are one of the countries that pollutes the most. With global warming, the melting of the polar areas is raising the level of the seas and oceans, and the phenomenon of lake cities such as New Orleans, in the United States, Naples in Italy and with some frequency the richest area of New York in lower Manhattan, are frequently being covered in water. The tsunami in Japan was an example of what nature can do, which will become a phenomenon to be repeated.

The United States has also been accused of polluting the outer space that surrounds the earth with a lot of garbage from its rocketry that is discarded at the end of its mission and that continues to float indefinitely, likewise Russia and China also pollute.

During the Republican period of Donald Trump, he irresponsibly once again granted a license to continue with coal exploitation and open new territories for the search for oil. But all of us are guilty for accepting these policies, giving the vote to such insensitive and ignorant rulers.

North America and the other great powers are still taking their time to address the problem of the Environment properly, they walk at a snail's pace, while we are already being victims of global warming, with the long and cold winter seasons and the high temperatures recorded in recent summers. An apostle of the environmental cause, is now Vice-President AL Gore Jr., Nobel Prize winner in 2007, who has dedicated himself with great enthusiasm to fighting global warming, promoted by many industry magnates with the exploitation of fossils. Al Gore has been traveling the world, raising awareness around the problem.

The United States is both a victim and a violator of global warming.

LIVE IN PEACE AND LET OTHERS LIVE IN PEACE

As long as the United States does not abandon its police role, as other powers in the world also want to do, the peace of the globe will always be threatened, as long as international conventions are not respected and the proliferation of nuclear weapons is prescribed, we will continue with the nightmare of radioactive mushrooms. Let us respect so that they also respect us.

It is the world body of the United Nations and its Security Council that is responsible for monitoring transgressors and taking the necessary measures, and not for any nation to unilaterally play the role of gendarme.

It is on the African Continent where coups d'état with adventurous military fortune hunters occurs, causing frequent massacres and destabilizing constitutional governments, there it is important that an organization such as the United Nations intervene to restore order.

The United Nations also has the task of certifying the conduct of nations in the event that they support drug dependency, the illicit trade in arms and drugs, the training of legionnaires to subvert order.

In the same way, it is this organization that is responsible for establishing Courts of Justice, where charges are filed against criminals against humanity, such as the group of former soldiers who tortured and killed the president of Haiti, in recent times, a those who prepared the conspiracy to destabilize a democratic government like Chile's or like the Cuban criminal with the surname Carriles who blew up a Cubana de Aviación passenger plane in 1976 and tried to blow up an auditorium with 2,000 students, simply because they were listening to Castro and was not tried. He remains at large despite being requested for various crimes in Venezuela and Cuba, the United States and some members of the island's colony in Miami, consider him a patriot, not a terrorist, so the qualifying term of a criminal, this subject to the geographical place where he commits the arbitrariness

There are many war criminals on the loose. It would be very important for the United Nations to carry out an in-depth investigation into who is responsible for the Covid 19 Pandemic and raise awareness of this problem, so that these terrible cases do not continue to be repeated. There are already many millions of victims around the world, the economic disaster around the globe that they have caused and so far, nothing is known about those responsible. According to experts, before the end of this century, some thirty million will die from the cause of Covid.

A nation with many prisons, with dangerous terrorists making destabilizing plans, with police forces applying order based on brutal methods and with large entertainment companies dedicated to glorifying violence, in which an exterminating gangster is worth more and is admired than a scientist or a poet, it becomes necessary and urgent to modify its political structures.

The United States, despite having been involved in several international wars due to the management of its policy, has been lucky that its territory has not been devastated as were: England, France, Germany, Russia, Poland and others. Both Russia, China and the United States are aware of how terrible and frightening a nuclear war would be with hydrogen bombs and all that rocketry with nuclear warheads pointing in all directions.

What has preserved world peace is the balance in the balance with atomic weapons, each of the powers has a number of bombs sufficient to destroy half the world and at the same time commit suicide, because other similar bombs are going to fall on it, there is a reciprocal fear, since the bombs that destroyed Hiroshima and Nagasaki represent only a percentage of less than 10% of destructive power, compared to the devastating capacity of today's bombs. Years ago, the powers in conflict kept flying super fortresses loaded with bombs, waiting for the order to unload them on already marked targets, since success consisted in getting ahead of the enemy, dropping them in minutes, now they are no longer planes, but rocketry and even fired from space bases with telephoto lenses or programmed drones that will come from everywhere.

When Nikita Khrushchev, in the sixties of the last century, ordered the dismantling of the nuclear platforms installed in Cuban territory, he commented that in any case, if the United States did not fulfill the agreed commitment, the bombs would take only a few seconds to shoot from their bases in Russia.

Making an exception to the terrorism of September 11, 2001, of Al Qaeda with the twin towers, the American population is unaware of the horror of seeing its territory bombed on a large scale and all its large buildings turned into ashes, as Hiroshima and Nagasaki experienced it before end the Second World War.

But the threats are everywhere, now it's North Korea, launching test rockets over international waters, testing the patience of neighboring nations to the limit; Russia whipping Ukraine with its enormous military power.

In my opinion, this is something that does not only concern a nation like North America, but all nations, when a punitive action of a country threatens to endanger world peace, because the radioactive clouds will be everywhere and there will be nobody to answer the red phone, and if many technicians activating the buttons of the directed rocketry.

But it is known that a few will survive, especially some world leaders who already have their underground rooms ready for their families, with their pantries stocked with caviar, vintage wines, Scotch spirits and potato chips. You and I, dear reader, are not on the guest list. When all this happens, since everything will have what they call the domino effect, only a few will be able to hear from a military man when he says again: Sorry, we were wrong again.

Mac Namara limited himself to acknowledging the big mistakes they made in Vietnam with a Sorry.

U.S.A: A WORLD OF GUNS

To preserve peace, it is necessary to maintain war.

Pentagon policy.

Unfortunately, one of the big businesses of this capitalist nation, for which it receives billions and billions of dollars, is the manufacture and sale of weapons; from hunting knives, to super fortresses, to bomb entire cities, tanks, drones and cannons of all calibers, machine guns, sophisticated rifles with telescopic sights, ammunition and ships, nuclear submarines and in general terms all the war paraphernalia of combat, available for the nation that has the financial means to buy it and training service personnel available, all of this is sold without further questions.

Oswald, the assassin of John F. Kennedy, only had to pay $23.00 for the rifle with a telescopic sight that he bought without having to show his face, by mail with which he killed the president. Donald Trump made a millionaire sale to Saudi Arabia, where Osama Bin Laden and many other terrorists were from.

Israel is a nation armed to the teeth, thanks to the United States that keeps it up to date with the most sophisticated, unfortunately they moved their capital from Tel Aviv to Jerusalem, now the holiest city in the world, seat of all the major religions, it is a minefield, full of soldiers and it is the eye of the hurricane, where great days of war are brewing, but at the same time it is an objective or target for other enemies such as the Palestinians.

Until recently, Jerusalem had been respected by the flow of tourists and by its sacred history where the relics of the main religions of the world are: The Jewish, Christian Catholic and Muslim with ancient temples. As the new capital of Israel, it makes it very vulnerable to its enemies.

Too bad, that the fields where the Master of Galilee preached peace, love and fellowship of the peoples, is now a nest of hawks with sharp claws.

As far as the United States of America is concerned, its great territory is a deadly pantry of supply and demand for all kinds of weapons with the highest technology constantly updated, the effects and results of which you can see in Hollywood movies.

There is also a large number of assault weapons, leg-breaking mines, hand grenades, revolvers of all calibers, easy to acquire, sometimes with just a driver's license and waiting about three days, while the rage passes, if who has an urge to kill a neighbor, they give him the option to repent. The children can corroborate how easy they are to operate, thanks to the fact that there are plastic imitation weapons for them, faithful copies of the authentic ones and of the ones that their daddy buys, and that he keeps in the closet. In Texas you can carry weapons without the need for permits or licenses, as if you lived in the years of the so-called Far West, recreated by Hollywood in cowboy movies, you just need to be over 18 years old and you can even buy a war tank.

Massacres in schools have proliferated for this reason as well in churches and markets. Some sensible people have thought that this broad policy of the ease of buying weapons should be reviewed, President Trump gave a solution that he considered better: arm teachers, so that they confront aggressive students.

Some families of blue blood and friends of racist supremacy, consider that children should be taught from an early age the use of weapons and the powerful corporation: National Rifle Association agrees with this, they see nothing wrong with this, everything invoking self-defense. We are not going to go very far, it is but to look at the number of videos and movies approved for children, where mass killings, exploding cars and vehicles, burning buildings and police cars turned into burning junk are glorified, all these ghastly terrorist visions witnessed, as the children prepare to go to school, eating their routine ration of cereal.

Do you, dear reader, consider that this is the best way to raise your children and that there is nothing wrong with these violent recreations of weapons, to feed the minds of children? If you accept it then don't be scared when the worst happens: Your child victim or victimizer.

For this reason, it is that I dare to describe this alienated and sick society with the use of weapons, seeing the number of coin-operated machines, recreating massacres, with characters who do not stop shooting. But all these products considered healthy entertainment are also exported to the nations with which we have trade.

On my last visit to Universal Studios, in Los Angeles, years ago I remember seeing a movie called: The Exterminator, at first, I thought it was a biography of Kissinger or something to kill cockroaches, but not the one that starred the ex-Two-term Governor of California, Arnold Schwarzenegger. From beginning to end, he activated death machines, constantly throwing fire, the bullets whistling over my head and around the sides of my ears, in such a realistic recreation that there were moments when I tried to leave the spectator's chair before such a sophisticated fantasy horror.

But there is also a lot of sexism, which really does not leave anything to the imagination, so what can we expect from this youth that is being formed in the 21st century, now they have added the most vulgar and rude dialogues because they consider that it is what the most of its people in real life. But you have to pay high prices if you want to stimulate your thrill-seeking mind.

It is obvious that the United States is not the only nation that sells and manufactures weapons, so do Russia, China, Great Britain, France, Australia and a considerable number of other nations, but the big deal is that these weapons within a short time they will be obsolete and there will be a need to replace them with the latest more sophisticated and deadlier models.

Gases or chemical weapons are also the order of the day, Syria has been the country to use them most recently; There are other types of gases used by the authorities to repress strikes and demonstrations, others more effective against crime.

The sale of lethal weapons throughout the world, by the great powers, including criminal governments, anti-democratic dictatorships, is done openly without hesitation or restriction. The United Nations should take control over them. Organized crime is the one that benefits the most, increasing every day the number of fatalities, surpassing that of terminal illnesses.

Having weapons is a symbol of power, it gives security to those who possess them, but at the same time it is a trap, it gives your children the opportunity to use it at any time or against those who look at you in a bad way or to answer a simple question. Rudeness and if you add a little alcohol to this, in less than a rooster sings, you will have to face the courts or be imprisoned.

The great powers usually sell sophisticated weapons to the countries that request them, some nations buy them to have the weapons they believe their armies need up to date, but these need to be operated by specialized technicians, which makes the sale more expensive by the time they finish pay the astronomical figures they are worth, they will already be obsolete, since the technology of weapons is modernized every day and is more deadly.

Latin America receives enormous quantities every year, because each one of them does not want to be left behind and although they lack other more necessary things, such as better machinery for agriculture, according to the criteria of the governments and their advisers, first there is what they call defense, even if they are not threatened or expecting an attack.

Irresponsibly, a Colombian president with the last name Santos, affiliated her with NATO without any danger. An organization that has nothing to do with public health, Colombia now has to pay 5 million euros from its limited national budget, money that could have been better invested in milk for school children, poor students.

Venezuela has empty supply markets, schools and hospitals do not have the necessary equipment, most things have to be imported, but when it comes to weapons there is a sufficiency that no one can imagine. The weapons, ammunition and trained personnel to repel any strike or protest is super modern. The arms culture is glorified by the media, television, videos and cinema, with a series of invincible characters that destroy an entire nation in seconds. A large percentage of the Venezuelan population has left the country, (approximately 10 million) seeking better opportunities and also for fear of repression, protesting is not allowed as in Cuba or Nicaragua and even less against the clique of soldiers that surround their president.

A housewife from Texas, ready to receive guests.

THE GREAT WAR MACHINERY OF THE U.S.A.

"War is big business: Invest your son!"

Folk Banner.

The destructive war power that the American Union now has, we cannot even imagine, even more so the secret weapons are many, they are ready there to be activated at the moment that the ruler of the day makes the decision, because there will be no time to that Congress meets to ratify it; weapons that are constantly being replaced by the latest, most sophisticated models. But the same happens with other powers, with which we do not get along very well, I imagine they will also be armed to the teeth. The latest news says that the deadliest will be activated from satellite stations. Some media report that the US military bases are approximately 800, located in 70 countries without counting those located in outer space.

Practically, since the United States was established as an independent nation of the British Empire in 1776, and for the last two hundred and fifty years, they have not stopped waging war throughout the world, inside and outside their territories. About two thousand conflicts without exaggeration; war exercises are part of their culture. There are hardly any countries with which they have not fought or at least been involved in their struggles in one way or another. The first battles were against the native Indians to take away their lands, after their civil war one of the bloodiest to eliminate slavery, the two world wars were presented, in which they participated, time after their expansionist conflicts imploring their Monroe Doctrine; others were those of Korea, Vietnam, Grenada, Iraq and Afghanistan.

With Latin America their incursions have not ceased, in many of them although they have not participated directly, they have promoted them as in the case of Chile. There are other silent wars that the American people are not aware of; there is a lot of war intelligence brainstorming future confrontations; it seems that we will not stop being occupied militarily, that is why the Pentagon, the great programmer, was created.

The largest economic budget goes to what they call defense, although no one is attacking us, new weapons are needed, their technology is voracious and insatiable, they cost an arm and a half, but in a short time they will be obsolete. The most expensive are the nuclear ones and that we no longer have deposits to store them. However, no one can accuse us of not wanting peace; if you want to find out how deadly they are, it is only to see the latest Hollywood movies. The only war America must wage is against poverty and pandemics.

Decades ago, a renowned former president Theodore Roosevelt said: "Speak softly but do not stop carrying the stick." However, he was the first politician to receive the Nobel Prize, which was ironic and Mohandas Gandhi, who advocated peace and promoter of Non-Violence, was ignored. Henry Kissinger received a Nobel Peace Prize for recommending saturation bombing in Asia and for planning the overthrow of Allende in Chile and the death of soldiers who opposed the Pinochet dictatorship.

Starting a war is very easy, the difficult part is ending it, but there is no need to worry because by then there will be no one on the globe, no thinking being who is concerned about these questions. The United States Army is everywhere, in strategic areas, waiting only for orders to intervene, other powers have the same. Militarism as it operates is a global calamity, in barracks polishing weapons, waiting for promotions and higher orders in exercises of aggressive strategy, with vulgar and loud-mouthed sergeants.

What would happen if these young people who are quartered, were taken out to take care of the streets, to provide social services, to educate gang members and keep them away from crime, to clean parks, highways and roads, to paint walls infected with graffiti, to collaborate in hospitals and health centers, to plant new trees, to monitor cities and popular neighborhoods, to be present without helmets and rifles in airports, to guide tourists and many other things that cost the government so much money to employ other workers, but without aggressive weapons?

It is necessary to modify the military concept, of so many young people living a conventual life, it would be better to prepare and guide them to live in peace and not for war. The concept of what was in the Kennedy era The Peace Corps with the so-called Alliance for Progress.

Soldiers with sophisticated rifles

IN DEFENSIVE TERMS, WHAT DO YOU CALL NATO?

In April 1949 a military organization was formed in Washington of which twelve countries were signatories, its name: North Atlantic Treaty Organization (NATO). Canada, France, Denmark, Belgium, Iceland, Italy, Luxembourg, Holland, Norway, Portugal, United States and England. A defensive pact by which the aggressor to any signatory nation will have to face all the others. The idea was also so that any attempt by the Soviet Union would have to think twice, in the same way it would discourage other nations from war purposes as well.

Three years later it was joined by other nations such as Greece and Turkey, later Germany entered the western sector and then Spain. Later other nations have been joining, until becoming a military power, very feared and difficult to challenge. In a way, what the United Nations could have controlled functions as an independent organization. NATO is controlled by a special council and its original headquarters was Paris, later they moved to Brussels, Belgium. Although this military monster may seem contradictory, of such great proportions at the global level, it has become a stabilizing force for peace that has prevented many conflicts.

Russia has been very concerned about the growth of the organization and the addition of nations such as Ukraine that belonged to the Soviet Union, but these countries are now seeking to benefit from new openings of Free Enterprise and not continue to be tied down, after the end of the so-called Block Soviet, which Putin plans to rebuild.

The fact that they join NATO, he would see as an outrageous and threatening act for his plans to reverse his dream of re-establishing a bloc of Pro-Soviet nations.

POLITICAL TERMINOLOGY A LITTLE CONFUSING

A large majority of people are unaware of political terms, due to their arbitrary use, for example in the case of Socialism and Nationalism, used by right and left parties throughout the ages. Adolf Hitler used these terms in Germany: NAZI National Socialism, in the thirties to awaken the patriotic spirit of an Aryan race that considered itself superior, after the defeat in the First World War and to which a series of impossible burdens were imposed to pay and leaving her in a very difficult prostration to recover; situation that he took advantage of two found a group of exalted, a more belligerent party that was coupled to the need, for this the: Nazi party (national socialist) emerged, with a swastika as a symbol.

It was also used by Benito Mussolini in Italy with fascism. National Socialist Party; before having dealed with the anarchist party and prepared his march on Rome with the black shirts.

Leftist political groups used it during the time they fought against the imperialist powers, Puerto Rico during the Albizu Campos era, trying to become independent from the United States, Cuba the same in its war against Spain. The communist party has used it by putting Marxism-Leninism before it. Fidel Castro in the 1960s used it in his famous declaration in Havana, proclaiming: "Our revolution is a Marxist-Leninist Socialist." Other political parties, although they do not consider themselves Marxists, use the term socialist like the liberals or independents, before putting the term democratic to create more impact, seeking populism.

Due to his exhaustion in using it inappropriately, the term socialist no longer inspires the fear it used to cause, considering it dangerous and revolutionary. Donald Trump accused the Democratic candidate, Biden, of being a socialist to scare many voters of the danger that he could represent in the event that he succeeded. The democratic left considered that what Trump did was a favor to Biden and that is why he triumphed. The term socialism, many politicians have shortened it, now they only say social, social-democratic, social-popular, social-Christian, social-republican or social-liberal. It would be interesting to ask those who have a confusion with the term socialism, to which of the two would they enroll: the Cuban left-wing type or the one who was a right-wing Nazi, fascist type? Today's Japan has also accepted the term socialist, very far from what communism was in its worst days with Stalin in government.

Fidel Castro speaking in the Plaza de la Revolución in Cuba

THE RELIGIOUS CONCEPTS

"God is dead".

Nietzsche.

"Nietzsche is dead."

God.

America can be considered a religious society, governed by the precepts of God. At least that is how it was proclaimed in its first declaration of independence, in its Constitution and in the first bills of circulating money: In God we trust, consecrated from the first days when this nation was forged, cutting all its ties with the British Empire and adopting the symbols and statements of Freemasonry.

Its first settlers from the colonies who landed on the Mayflower, in 1620, were pilgrims, missionaries, Puritans and Quakers fleeing religious intolerance and many more merchants and adventurers in search of new opportunities in the colonies of America, but with them came also ministers Protestants and Calvinists of various denominations to continue their pastoral work with the same orthodox intolerances and intransigence in their country of origin, persecuting those who practiced the magical arts, witchcraft, sorcery and esotericism. They soon established courts to prosecute them and condemn them to the stake and anyone who wanted to get rid of their enemies, just had to accuse them of diabolical practices and invent some evidence and these people were sentenced to death.

Hollywood has found in these historical events a very blockbuster theme to exploit the curiosity of the crowds, recreating trials, hangings and human bonfires.

the great awakening, was a religious movement that originated in America in 1730, in the territories called New England, it was a series of acts and sermons preached by a charismatic minister Jonathan Edwards and another Anglican missionary named George Whitefield, who were acting as Christian evangelizers in rural areas from Maine to Georgia, on a voluntary basis, outside the context of the church, promoting teachings and reaffirming the ways of salvation, who had a great impact in what would soon be the territory of the United States , which in a certain way helped to promote a certain religious tolerance in the different existing churches with other denominations such as that of the first Puritans, who came with the doctrines of Luther and Calvin, who influenced many government acts and challenged with the New Protestant Bible , those already existing of the Roman Pope, who ruled in the Vatican States, the Christian authority nab

Max Weber was a German sociologist who in 1904 wrote an essay: The Protestant Ethic and The Spirit of Capitalism, in which he argued as a fact that the Protestant principles were those that contributed to the development and growth of commerce and industry in the economy. Capitalist where the nation should be headed.

From the beginning in North America, it was Protestantism and Calvinism that laid the religious foundations; to the south and west were the Spaniards in the territory claimed by Mexico, the monks and missionaries imposed the Catholic religion with the Bull granted by the Spanish Pope Alexander VI, of the Borgias family and that consecrated Fernando de Aragón and Isabel de Castilla: The Catholic Monarchs, creators in turn of The Holy Office, with the friar Tomas de Torquemada, the infamous Inquisition that sacrificed so many victims on racks in Spain and the colonies of America, but also the Protestants in their colonies, they did the same, persecuting the opponents of their faith, such as infidel atheists and witches, and condemning them to the gallows and the stake in orgies of persecution in the darkest age that the so-called New World has ever had.

Although the state of the American union in more recent times has not accepted any religion as official, Protestantism from the beginning has maintained a supremacy in the number of churches and faithful followers. The church for its part as an attached institution is in solidarity with the capitalist system: Status Quo.

The freedom of religious practices is highly respected by the state, since the first heroes of the nation entrusted it to God and endorsed it in their constitutional acts.

Pastors and ministers of all churches operate with great freedoms

RELIGION IS THE OPIUM OF PEOPLE

Karl Marx.

Karl Marx predicted the end of all religions, when the government of the proletariat triumphed, I do not consider that within his party there would be a struggle for power with its managers: Lenin and Stalin and the generation that preceded him, who by their authoritarianism, what they were propitiating was their own burial, the Soviet people were already tired of so many totalitarian dictatorships and sought to breathe with something new. The religion in Russia continued with its orthodox churches but not belligerent and in that case its beautiful onion-head churches and cathedrals have been respected by all faiths. Both the church and the state have respected each other's jurisdiction, without interfering in each other's affairs.

In America, the diversity of existing beliefs has made the state modify many of its statements to respect a certain neutrality. The prayer that was done in the schools was suppressed, but the cult of the flag continues, as well as the swearing on the bible in the presidential office and the truthfulness of the word before the courts; perjury is a punishable offense. The name of God is still invoked by many at the time of taking food, when starting sporting events and inaugurating works and starting businesses, even fraudulent ones. Some Catholic Popes have made various attempts to seek a rapprochement with the Russian Hierarchs, but nothing has happened.

Another thing that is important to mention as an incongruous reality is the voluntary segregation in the American churches, the blacks have their temples where the rite acquires a preponderance with the song, the cadenced movements and cataleptic states appear continuously. Although it is not forbidden in black churches, whites do not show up even if they have the same religion and vice versa.

Martin Luther King Jr. was a charismatic minister of a church in Montgomery, Alabama, who distinguished himself for his political leadership among blacks and with a program of non-violence, like the one preached by Gandhi in India, Nelson Mandela in the South Africa, and Jorge Eliecer Gaitán in Colombia, before he was assassinated. Luther King Jr. led many protests for Civil Rights, with remarkable success, which earned him the Nobel Prize and worldwide recognition, although he was blacklisted as a terrorist and imprisoned several times by Edgard Hoover.

Returning to the role of religion in America, within its political and social development, it is important to recognize that it functions as an institution for ethics and morals in the world development of a democratic and civil society, with numerous beliefs and aspects. In some sects, there are African voodoo rites, which sacrifice black cats and roosters with Santeria that is practiced privately, there is even an evangelizing church with the satanic bible that officiates a black mass in San Francisco, California. A frequently robbed Baptist church posted a notice on its front door: Assailants caught in the act will be baptized: Trespasser Will be baptized.

All churches are exempt from taxes, particularly because they preach obedience, comply with the law, pay taxes and respect the rights of others. Evangelization is allowed outside the churches; many ministers have obtained large capitals in religious promotions and in campaigns combined with political acts. They do a multitude of businesses with real estate, sale of shares, telephone collections, they put many people to work, as volunteers and without having to pay taxes or be accountable to the state.

A prosperous church has been called: Scientology today a millionaire entity with thousands of volunteers, it is a privilege to belong to it, its training courses are expensive and with modern and high-tech facilities, although it operates as a university that grants degrees, its directors They present it as just another religion. It is important to clarify that this church does not have religious rites, does not collect public alms and its directors are not clergymen with ranks of power, but rather executives.

There are others that are a little more conventional, not so ostentatious with their gospel, practices and rites that operate with a multitude of volunteer workers-servants, but their ministers are practically businessmen and businessmen.

Some of them, already millionaires with their own radio and television stations like LA CBN: Pat Robertson's Christian Broadcasting Network, a minister dressed very elegantly as a company manager, but with expensive cowboy boots, who in 1966, was close to Richard Nixon, who talked to God every day and who maintained that the supreme maker had made him rich and powerful to lead his flock. Pat Robertson came to propose the assassination of Venezuelan commander Hugo Chavez.

He has always been behind the presidency of the nation with his 700 CLUB, in 1977, he published a book with the name of The New World Order and has considered himself a member of the so-called Illuminati, a chosen few who control the federal reserves, the banks, politics and militarism.

Jerry Falwell has been another important figure among the millionaire ministers who have become famous as owners of large media, to spread their Baptist religion in the state of Virginia and was very famous since 1978, it is said that he was going to be the second Billy Graham. Falwell as Pat Robertson maintained that he also talked to God every day and asked for advice on how to be successful.

Another colorful character in the North American churches was Jim Bakker, who in 1987 established his economic empire, in the company of his wife Timmy with his television station and used the money of the parishioners to forge a great fortune, he also had several scandals with prostitutes to the who paid for his silence. Although the justice sentenced him for these crimes to 45 years, after having paid 10 years in prison, and a fine of half a million dollars, he has managed to get out again and re-mount his TV shows: Slate and new account. Justice in religious terms has been very tolerant with these so-called shepherds of God.

Billy Graham was a pastor who filled an entire religious cycle in America with great worldwide recognition, visited many countries and fostered a rapprochement with Jewish and Russian Orthodox doctrine, he was a great friend of Martin Luther King Jr. and his presentations were well attended, He died a few days before his 100th birthday. In religious matters he was the number one figure and left a legacy within his very respectable church.

Other ministers of various churches have fallen into corrupt acts and have been condemned by justice. As a great incentive to make a fortune, the proliferation of churches has prospered epidemically, even in garages with many statements and denominations, particularly called: Christian; Salvadorans in Latino communities have taken the lead.

The Catholic Church, on the other hand, so prosperous and numerous at one time, has lost many of its faithful due to its orthodoxy and intransigence for not accepting the new changes. Empty convents, churches, schools and colleges are proof of their problems; the tolerated and hidden pederasty of many of its vicars is being highly questioned. Also, the Catholic Church continues with its opposition to birth control and condom use as a condom, you can have many children without limit, abortion is not accepted under any circumstances, even if the mother is in danger of death.

However, the American government maintains excellent relations with the Vatican and several Popes have been received with great protocol. During the republican reign of Ronald Reagan, although he was not a Catholic, he maintained a good friendship with Pope Paul II, Karol Wojtyla, as a Polish citizen, what came to be called the holy alliance and received a lot of financial aid to form the liberation movement: Solidarity, which managed to defeat communism in Poland and begin the dismantling of the Marxist structures. Reagan and Obama visited the Pope in Rome, even though they were not Catholic during their terms. In political matters, John Paul II was an arrogant religious, he did not tolerate social movements, nor any progressive changes, ultra-conservative and hard-liner.

Paul II had excellent relations with Kissinger, Pinochet, Videla and the Argentine military junta and other Caribbean tyrants, from whom he accepted tributes and honors. He never condemned the pederasty of bishops and vicars, despite having known many cases, decreeing a curtain of silence.

Nor did he protest when Roberto Dawison, president of El Salvador, had Bishop Romero assassinated by a military elite while he was officiating a mass, because the spoke of a social church. However, the Pope was sanctified by the Vatican.

Paul II had a reign of 27 years, becoming the first to break with the line of Italian Popes maintained for 455 years within Catholic orthodoxy, he distinguished himself for being a very traveling prelate, in 1979 he visited the United States and had a great Reception in the great Hispanic community, with a pleasant smile he conquered many followers, but in political matters he was very arrogant, he did not have the humility of John XXIII, nor the austerity that has distinguished the current Pope Francis. The Polish Pope died in 2005, he was the victim of an attack in the square near the Vatican, but he managed to recover, he was succeeded by another of German origin who in his youth was in the Nazi militias and now for the first time we have one of Latin origin: Argentine of the Jesuit community, simple, humble and with an open mind, truly an exception as was John XXIII.

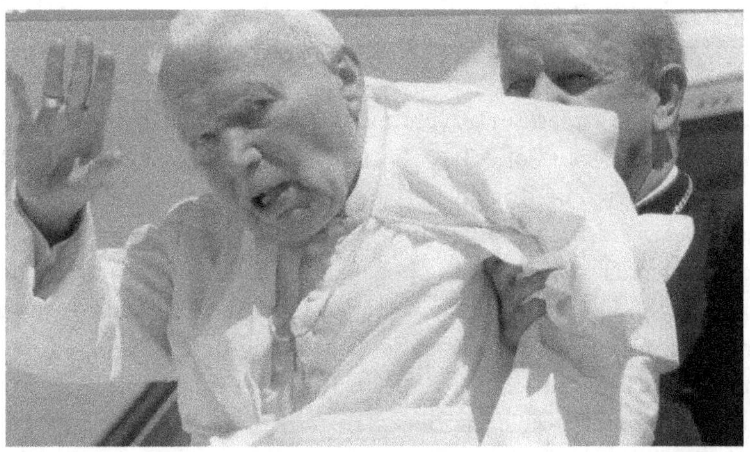

Juan Pablo II

Virtually in America there has also existed since 1900, a separation of church and state, adopted by the Supreme Court of Justice. Particularly in schools, it became very notorious when it was declared unconstitutional in June 1963, the reading of the bible and religious prayers at the beginning of classes.

Some Protestant churches have achieved great preponderance and their ministers have taken advantage of certain freedoms to take personal advantage as tycoons and businessmen controlling media such as radio and television stations, making religious and political proselytism with daily presentations, and have not only accumulated great fortunes, but they have also starred in scandals that are public knowledge, due to denunciations among themselves for the desire to capture positions, many of them corroborated by their own confessions before large audiences in which theatrically as actors they have mourned their sins with great repentance, in which that shameful conduct on prostitution, payments to silence witnesses, extortion and appropriation of millionaire funds to support personal luxuries has come to the surface.

The United States has been very respectful of religious jurisdiction, allowing cults of all kinds to be established, without interfering or investigating their background, for this reason cases such as that of the psychopath David Koresh were presented in Waco, Texas in February 1993 , in which 76 members of the religious sect died: 19 men, 34 women and 23 children, as a result of a fire in the buildings that functioned as the religious center of the Seventh-day Adventist Church, where Koresh locked himself up to confront the FBI-ordered firearms investigation. Considering himself the messiah, he challenged the guards of order, producing a confrontation in which there were several explosions with tragic and unfortunate results.

A tragedy that no one will forget, the death of 918 parishioners by suicide, ordered by pistol by Pastor James Warren Jones, who forced them to drink cyanide on November 18, 1978 in Jamestown, Guyana and then he committed suicide with a firearm, this minister of the evangelical church had taken refuge in South America with numerous followers who followed him to found a town to perpetuate the ego with the name of the pastor.

In March 1970 a small congregation by the name of Gates of Heaven, Heavies Gate, proclaimed themselves descendants of Jesus Christ in San Diego County, California, its founders a couple consisting of Marshall Applewhite and Bonnie Nettles. They isolated themselves and cut relationships with family and friends, quit their jobs and distributed all their belongings and prepared for a great trip in a spaceship, after they ordered the 39 members, who made up the sect, who considered themselves messengers, to commit suicide. Divine, assiduous readers of the Bible and all literature related to aliens, the UFO and with the certainty that the world would disappear.

They also thought that they were the chosen ones to populate other planets and colonize them, also renouncing their sexuality, for which some members of the sect previously traveled to Mexico to be castrated.

At that time, the date of the passage of Comet Hale-Bopp coincided, every 75 years, and its directors were convinced that it was proof of the arrival of the aliens and the time to leave with them in March 1997, for which they rented a large mansion in San Diego County. A devotee of the brotherhood would take care of all the details and continue letting know the latest news and developments of the sect. The authorities were notified and they showed up to take the bodies of the suicide bombers to the morgue. The members who were rigorously dressed in black with their respective ties and Heaven's Gate Away Team tags.

There are many sects and religious brotherhoods in America, some that privately commit many outrages and improper acts, protected by the "Freedom of Worship." We would occupy many pages if we recounted how they succeed in attracting new followers, sometimes assaulting their good faith and pretending that they do what is best for them.

Taking stock of the contribution of religions to the aggrandizement of the nation in ethics, morals, exemplary conduct, spirituality and humanism, this has been very poor with very rare exceptions, throughout history, we owe practically nothing to these Pastors or on the contrary, ministers have taken advantage of the circumstances and taken advantage of the status that has been granted to them.

THE CONGLOMERATION OF ETHNIC GROUPS IN AMERICA AND ITS CONTRIBUTION TO DEVELOPMENT

***The black community*:**

With the increase of slavery in colonial times, the black race was one of the ethnic groups that contributed with their work to the economic development of this nation, enduring hunger, misery and in the worst human conditions based on the whip, particularly in the southern states: Georgia, Alabama and Mississippi, in the cotton crops, also in the hardest tasks of the large farms, the same in the mines. Many blacks were forced to fight in favor of maintaining slavery by order of their masters and lords in the bloody Civil War. As for the children of slaves, they were also born slaves and from a very young age they were forced to work, those who went to school were segregated, only until the 50s of the last centuries did this discrimination end, on the part of the Supreme Court of Justice, but for its implementation it took many more years, the churches kept this segregation.

The Abolitionism that appears in 1830, emerges from the evangelical movement of Protestantism in residents of the north of the nation, pacifists and most of all proclaimed by women, three decades before the civil war, its philosophy is theological with the conviction that slavery was a sin.

Many people tend to believe that slavery originated in Africa and that their black community was the first to be enslaved. This practice appears in history, almost at the same time that the first disputes between nations arise, who used the defeated armies for the rough trades of agriculture, construction. In Egypt thousands worked in the pyramids, also in the monuments of Greece and Rome, but they were not only black. The Bible speaks that the son of the Prophet Noah was sold as a slave to some merchants. Others speak of the Curse of Ham.

It was the Portuguese who started the slave trade in the eastern and western regions of Africa and the Dutch in the south, establishing trade and marketing, particularly where the European colonies were, around the year 1400 and 1600, with the traffic of large ships along the west coast, with itineraries also through the Caribbean colonies, serving where the large crops of tobacco, sugar and coffee were.

It is estimated that this traffic of blacks reached ten million in these plantations, many were destined for the North American colonies.

After the civil war and the end of slavery, blacks gradually began to integrate into different kinds of jobs and small businesses and in 1865 a racial wave awoke, with the purpose of stopping their progress. A group of white ex-combatants of the Civil War, belonging to veterans of the army, which functioned as a Social Club, with its maximum leader: General Nathan Bedford Forrest, massacred 300 black soldiers at Fort Pillow in Tennessee, without any excuse, and I initiate a series of criminal incursions against them with the organization of the Ku Klux Klan born in Pulaski, in the south with white uniforms and some mounted on horseback, in the years that were considered to be the reconstruction, preventing them from participating in politics. In view of the multiple and frequent criminal acts against blacks, the government only until 1871, Congress passed a law by Ulysses Grant to use the forces of the army to stop the Klan raids, making them stop the lynchings.

In 1915, the KKK, the Klan, was resurrected in Georgia as a fraternal organization of gentlemen, expanding its network of persecution against other organizations of immigrant Jews and Catholics, those who suffered persecution and lynching, like blacks, in order to establish a racial purge, such as the that Hitler implanted in 1933 in Germany.

It was the time of frequent lynchings, the victims were taken from their homes as if they were wild beasts and publicly burned as human torches, as in ancient Rome, because the perpetrators had a license to kill, they did not even respect the churches, the show ended burning a large cross in downtown areas, gave the impression that they were the same authorities appointed to maintain order, according to the chronicles of the time, these orgies of blood and cannibalism, did not seem executed by human beings and there are no epithets to describe this conduct.

Although the KKK Klan disappeared for a time, decades later like the Phoenix they resurfaced sporadically with infrequent acts, so that they would not be forgotten, but always emphasizing white supremacy, with the model: THE SUPER MAN created by Federico Nietzsche, the German philosopher in his work THUS SPEAK ZARATHUSTRA, adopted by Adolf Hitler in his theory MY STRUGGLE.

The American racists forgot that blacks were the ones who have worked the most for the aggrandizement and development of the nation, first as slaves in the fields of agriculture, later in factories, mines and in the cities as servants and as soldiers in the wars, defending interests alien to their own condition.

During the years of the 1914s a prominent black leader, Marcus Garvey, who dressed as a great military man proposed the idea of a return to African lands, met with his powerful founding enemy of the KKK, Nathan Belfort in an Atlanta Georgia motel, in view of the growing racist wave that was welcomed by a large number of victims of the black community, especially those who remained almost as slaves, poorly paid, segregated and hated by whites. But the first to protest were the more racists, owners of large farms and ranches and entrepreneurs of large factories and industries, for fear of an increase in labor prices and services. But a scapegoat was also needed to justify their conduct against black ethnic groups.

It was the moment in which new concepts and ideas arose around the existing injustices, an awareness, there was talk of reforms to the laws, of establishing compensation for the victims, of giving more opportunities to the families of impoverished and subjugated workers and to stop once and for all THE BLACK HOLOCAUST.

Then political leaders appeared in the community to demand that these promises be made a reality in 1989 and 1990, Randall Robinson and John Conyers stood out for introducing reforms and laws in favor of the new programs that facilitated these compensations and who later gave the initiative so that the fight for the Civil Rights of blacks appeared. Martin Luther King Jr., with his philosophy of "nonviolence" for his dedication to these ideals, was assassinated, which the black leader Stokely Carmichael considered that the white community had declared war on the black community, then others followed victims of intolerance like Malcolm X among the Muslim community.

Born into slavery, Frederic Douglas was a noted social reformer, abolitionist, orator, and writer who is also remembered for his contributions as a multi-faceted statesman. Booker T. Washington also appears in his day as a prominent leader and educator and was the author of Up from Slavery.

The only place where the black was not discriminated against was in the ranks of the army where he was offering his life, defending interests other than his own destiny.

Already in the decades of the 50s, 60s and 70s the black community woke up from its stagnation and began to respond to violence with violence. Groups like THE BLACK PANTHERS appeared in popular neighborhoods organizing legionnaires for the cause, burning down even their own ghettos and organizing themselves politically to confront their armed struggle.

Eldridge Claver was a prominent figure as the Peace and Freedom Party candidate for the Black Panthers, author of the book Soul on Ice, written in prison.

One of the most spectacular actions took place in San José California, when several leaders of the Black Panthers were tried in full court, managing to kidnap the judge with weapons provided by the activist Angela Davis and caused several deaths, including Judge and the accused. Bobby Séale, Huey Newton, and George Jackson, the latter of whom was shot in prison by his guards at San Quentin. There was violence in the big cities and confrontations with the authorities, creating highly dangerous areas such as Watts in Los Angeles, the streets of Chicago and Harlem in New York.

Police brutality as a force of order has caused many victims and the state has been forced to compensate with large sums for this reprehensible behavior.

An important fact worth remembering in history, during the tenure of Abraham Lincoln and long before the end of the civil war, on January 1, 1865 based on acts of Congress, Lincoln made what was called THE PROCLAMATION DE LA EMANCIPACIÓN, by which the properties of those who would return the slaves to their owners would be confiscated, although the confederate states did not give freedom to the slaves, approximately four million of them, until the union was sealed and the victory in April 1865.

Although there is no total integration, white supremacy is still very powerful, managing to control the most important positions, but not as important as in 1800. The so-called "people of color" have managed to win a large number of jobs within the official bureaucracy and within the police. In the post offices they practically have 80 percent. The great black community through the ages has managed to stand out in the field of sports and entertainment. In 1936, a black athlete, Jesse Owens, was covered in glory at the German Olympics against Hitler himself, a supporter of Aryan supremacy who had to acknowledge his victory over a large number of white athletes. Owens was also noted with the famous Harlem Globetrotters.

Blacks in boxing have always maintained a superiority, such is the case of Jack Johnson in 1910 who was crowned World Champion of all weights, Joe Louis was another spectacular fighter, Mahatma Ali achieved it in more recent years by beating Sony Ribbon.

Regarding the field of music, it is said of a black New Orleans pianist Ferdinand Morton Jelly Roll, who was the creator of Jazz and his recordings were made with a band called Red Hot Peppers years before 1930, after they stood out Duke Ellington, Thomas Walker, Eubie Blake, Jessie Smith, Louis Armstrong, later their most notable figures moved to gangs in New York Harlem, Chicago and Los Angeles.

Blue Grass was another very important music within what was also called Country Blues in the 1930s, which achieved great notoriety among black people. Dancers, singers, interpreters, band musicians began to saturate the entertainment environment with great success, it was the glorious time in which the singer and dancer born in the slums of St. Louis Illinois, Josephine Baker, at just 13 years old, He traveled to France and lived in Paris, becoming a famous vaudeville star, with his Revue Negre, with his erotic and semi-nude creations, he caused a great sensation in the famous FOLIIES BERGERE.

For his part SATCHMO, Louis Armstrong another great jazz star in New Orleans with his cornet was also becoming a notable figure not only in Chicago but also Harlem New York in bands like Hot Five and Hot Seven, creating a very particular style with Ella Fitzgerald, his greatest success was achieved when he filmed Hello Dolly and sang in a duet with Barbra Streisan. Other jazz stars included Tadd Dameron, Thelonious Monk, Kenny Clark, Dizzy Gillespie, John Coltrane, Joy Flip Phillips, Miles Davis. Bessie Smith was crowned Queen of the Blues. In Las Vegas, Nevada, Sammy Davis Jr. was a star figure in entertainment and film alongside Frank Sinatra.

Radio, cinema and television opened wide the doors to blacks and it was when the union of inter-racial couples became very notorious. Boxers, baseball players were well known in the so-called dance of the millions. It was the turn of the blacks for the great revenge and they began to charge dearly and stomp their feet on the red carpets.

Marcus Garvey founded in Jamaica an association for the betterment of the black community, with a series of commercial missionary and Christian purposes for education and in 1916 he moved to the United States, winning many successes for his intelligence and oratory, Bob Marley and Malcon X admired him very much. In 1905 a group of black intellectuals created the Niagara Movement, including W.E.B. Du Bois for civil rights and the advancement of people of color.

Marian Anderson famous black contralto was another of the notable figures in the world of music, with great resonance in Europe, Jean Sibelius wrote a piece for her: SOLITUDE, but in America she was denied entry to Constitution Hall, in 1939 in Washington by a racist society, but later President Roosevelt's wife, Eleanor, arranged for her a presentation at the Lincoln Memorial before an audience of 75,000 music lovers, later it was presented at the Metropolitan Opera House in New York. In terms of politics, black women have had a great performance in recent years, such is the case of Condoleezza Rice during the Bush administration as Secretary of State.

The idea of a great America cannot be conceived without the participation of the black race, proof of this, of its capabilities in all fields of intelligence, the emergence of a figure like Obama as the first black President among so many renowned figures in the Democratic Party, even more his re-election in a second period and with a high percentage of popularity, is an irrefutable proof of his competence before the first magistracy, it is also corroborated that a character like Donald Trump of the Aryan race, multimillionaire, does not He achieved the second period and with a powerful aggressive machinery that managed to invade the Capitol grounds in retaliation, in which there were several deaths, supported by the support of his Republican party.

It is important to keep in mind that racism, hatred against the black population has also existed, supported by the ruling classes, white elites in much of Latin America and has patented several slogans, slogans against them: "Black who does not do evil to the input, it makes it to the output. The only good black is the dead black. In the same way, racist hatred has spread against the native Indian, entire communities for centuries have been persecuted and dispossessed of their lands, even in modern times, with the consent of governments that consider themselves Christian.

In Argentina, entire communities of indigenous natives were exterminated at different times, considering them as beasts that did not deserve to live. In the late nineteenth century in the so-called Desert Campaign. In the Chaco region there were massacres against the Mapuches in order to take away their lands, history cites people like Julio Argentino Roca, awarded with his effigy on the banknotes in circulation, as well as Juan Manuel Blanes.

Eldridge Cleaver

Jesse Jackson

Stokely Carmichael

Frederick Douglas

Angela Davis

Rosa Parks

Marian Anderson

Elaine Brown

Ku Klux Klan: American white supremacist hate group.

THE BROWN PEOPLE: LA RAZA DE BRONZE LOS LATINOS, THEIR IMPORTANT CONTRIBUTION

Since the time of the conquest, when Spain at the end of 1400 brought about the arrival of the first navigators such as Cristoforo Colombo, an Italian with the promise of finding a shorter way to the East, it opened wide its prisons to complete its crews of the ships bound for an unsuspected world, most of them criminals and adventurers with the option of achieving an unlikely freedom. This is how the islands of the Caribbean, Florida, California, Texas and other states were populated, accompanied by some Catholic missionaries. Further north came English and French settlers with a Protestant and Calvinist clergy. North America had Hispanic communities from very early times, later due to its proximity to Mexico, there was always a flow of immigrants, in addition to those who populated the territories that it obtained through purchases and the spoils of bloody wars. They say that Francisco Villa led a punitive raid in order to take over the United States, but his colleagues convinced him that if he won, he would have to support a million gringos, so he gave up and returned to his town.

For work in the fields in agricultural areas, as the black population, the Latino has become a very important labor force, as did the native Indians in colonial times with the Spanish missionaries, to achieve the development of the large haciendas and farms, in towns with many Hispanic names, taken from Catholic saints such as San José, San Luis, San Pedro, San Francisco, San Onofre, San Diego, San Joaquín, Los Angeles, Santa Clara, Santa Barbara, etc. When the United States won the territorial war against Mexico and managed to integrate the five southern states into the union, they promised to respect some inalienable rights, through the Guadalupe Hidalgo treaty, among what they solemnly swore was to respect the use of Spanish as their native language, permanence of the inhabitants who wished it under other laws, accept their customs, as a legacy and others, but years later they forgot to comply with them, speak another language Other than English, it was not allowed in schools, factories, and other venues. Ronald Reagan during his term, was very strict and intolerable, he ended many programs that favored Latinos in the field of education, as a member of the Republican Party he fought bilingualism.

In politics, he was always in favor of sponsoring right-wing dictatorships to curb socialist ideas, establishing dictatorships such as that of Castillo Armas in Guatemala and invading territories such as Grenada in the Caribbean and sponsoring incursions such as those of the Iran Contras in Nicaragua, and supporting satraps like the Panamanian dictator Manuel Antonio Noriega, in a season in which he played a double role as an informant agent for the CIA and figurehead of the most powerful drug lords. Noriega was overthrown in a Marine raid on Panama, thus ending his orgy of terror and misrule.

Democratic President J. Carter, during his government, returned to Panama the rights to the Canal, in the time of Torrijos in an act of justice that was highly applauded.

In the Hispanic community, especially in the field of agriculture, a leader stood out who managed to organize Mexican-Americans, his name was Cesar Chavez, originally from Arizona, from working families in the fields, founder of the National Farm Workers Association, whose activities began in 1962, especially with the grape pickers, their frequent boycotts in favor of better wages and humanistic treatment for their peons shook the national conscience in their favor. Sometimes he used as a banner the image of the Virgin of Guadalupe in the San Joaquin Valley. He had a good friendship with Robert Kennedy who visited him several times in his agricultural fields, in solidarity with his cause. Chavez at his early death left a generous and humble legacy, worthy of imitation for his dedication in favor of the needy, something similar to Martin Luther King Jr. with his ideas of Non-violence.

During the sixties, there was a lot of political agitation in the minorities, due to racist problems and particularly in the gestures, neighborhoods considered to be workers and peasants. In East Los Angeles, where CHICANISM emerged with great momentum, particularly in the Mexican community. Possibly the term Chicano, was adopted from the Mesoamerican inhabitants Mechicas or Mexicas. Nahualtecas who had their settlement in the great Valley of Mexico.

Although in the United States there is a large group of Mexican immigrants and many other Mexican Americans, the idea of a political party of Chicanos that was born in the sixties with Reyes Tijerina, has not prospered. In the universities of the southern states, they have chairs such as CHICANO STUDIES that have replaced Spanish courses, with Mexican-American professors and intellectuals such as Rolando Hinojosa, Sandra Cisneros, Rodolfo Anaya, Roberto Haro, Rodolfo Corky Gonzalez and another large group of educators in colleges and elementary schools.

Radio and television stations, like some journalists, have been controlled by Mexican tycoons. A pioneer of radio in Spanish in the twenties was Pedro J, Gonzalez, a great fighter for Mexican rights who were discriminated against, became a citizen to be able to do his job better, however he was imprisoned and deported.

Movies and television made in his memory a funny character Speedy Gonzalez, like a fast mouse who spoke Spanglish and did mischief, was ostracized and forgotten despite his great popularity.

There is also another series of fantastic legends around what has been called AXTLAN with roots also in the stories of the Mexicas, of a rich territory similar to El Dorado or the seven cities of Cíbola in the north of the Aztec country, which they say was called Mexcaltitlan., legends made known by a friar named Diego Duran in 1581.

There are now a large number of people claiming their ancestor from Aztlan, located in I don't know where, possibly in the Alien paradise, which has no relation or resemblance to North America or Mexico.

A large majority of Latinos have remained in the ranks of the Democratic Party, where they feel more comfortable, and have risen to prominent positions in government in different administrations. A very important distinction was the appointment of a Mexican-American as treasurer, Romana Bañuelos, today the Latino power cannot be denied in terms of votes; they can decide presidential terms and legislative entities and even the most ultra-conservative recognize it, that's why at the time of elections, they become great missionaries making sweet promises, trying to capture votes, which only last the election season.

When those million Spanish-speakers, who have been waiting a long time for their legalization, are able to catch up and acquire their citizenship, it is not uncommon for a Latino politician to give us a big surprise at the White House. Until recent years, Antonio Villaraigosa, Henry Cisneros, Julián Castro and Marco Rubio have stood out as officials.

In all the wars in which North America has been involved, Latin American residents have participated, putting their chests to the bullets, responding to the obligations contracted as citizens or residents, in the Second World War Korea, Vietnam, Iraq and Afghanistan, even in the punitive raids in Latin America by the CIA.

The Republican Party has shown itself to be a defender of the interests of the rich, in which the most recalcitrant ultra-conservative racists are grouped, who favor authoritarian governments, friends of warmongering and intolerance. It seems inconceivable, although they hate minorities, one cannot explain how there can be blacks, Asians and Latinos who support that party so alien to the interests of the neediest. Voting for your own executioners is a kind of masochism. Something similar to the time that blacks were forced to fight in favor of maintaining slavery.

In recent times, the United States has used its Department of Immigration and Naturalization as a kind of filter to stop an unstoppable wave of undocumented immigrants from Central and South America, which has become a terrible nightmare, based on the fact that many governments of these nations want to get rid of the problem of overpopulation, social struggles, wars, unemployment and famines, the solution for them is to encourage the exodus at any cost and particularly to the United States, hoping that these quickly obtain work and receive a flow of dollars , with remittances to their relatives, they have even opened prisons to get rid of dangerous criminals, forcing them to emigrate and giving them documentation that makes the trip to the American Paradise possible.

Before, no one could leave the country without documentation from these Central American nations, now the intention of starting to walk north with the purpose of sending dollars to their country of origin is enough. But much of this dream is nothing more than a death trap for these desperate gangs; an uncertain event awaits them along the way: famines, diseases, extortion by drug traffickers, robberies for their few savings, deadly epidemics, rapes and criminal acts and ultimately death.

A large percentage will not make it, they will die on the way, and they will lose their children or other members of their family, which is why they have adopted traveling in large groups to overcome dangers together. The four horsemen of the apocalypse await them on the road with their skeletal nags to greet them.

Chilling number of potential Latino migrants arriving in the United States.

Cesar Chávez

Reyes Tijerina. Chicano leader

Peasant being searched for weapons

LET MY PEOPLE GO: LET MY PEOPLE PASS

(Let them eat cake)

Marie Antoinette in the French Revolution, on her way to the guillotine

Looking dispassionately at the problem of stampede-type human waves and with a more humanistic and Christian sense, these beings who are called by some: "The forgotten of God", in a desperate attempt to save their lives from so much injustice in which they live , of so much corruption and violence of their governments, they are not to blame for seeking a better future for themselves and their children and with a few savings, they are fleeing from that mistreatment, from the lack of opportunities and in search of that Northern Paradise, not only as a fleeting adventurer from other times, but in large groups, with their minor children and others in their arms, pregnant women sometimes in an advanced state of pregnancy; in the most extreme conditions of poverty, hoping to walk the thousands of miles that separate them from the enormous wall that now exists with very high spirits and imploring "Help us, my God!" Another kind of Wailing Wall, on the border of the United States and Mexico, like the one that exists in Jerusalem.

The Latino community in North American cities has become a labor force in charge of the roughest and worst paid services, in bakeries, restaurants, hospitals, gardeners, car washes, caretakers, factory workers, workshops, park cleaning, some people They employ undocumented immigrants in domestic tasks with salaries lower than the minimum stipulated, without the benefits required by law.

The demand of these undocumented immigrants exceeds those who already work with work permits with great tolerance by the authorities, thus the government saves millions of dollars in labor benefits, in terms of visas and permits there is a large business with false papers circulating, a never-ending problem, supplied by the underworld and drug dealers. The immigration department remains very active and every day there are new arrests of what they call "wet", a term applied to those who crossed the Rio Grande swimming, on the border with Mexico, deportations are made almost every day, but many They return in a short time, taking advantage of what they have learned in tricks and skills to jump the fence and evade the authorities.

Within the existing problem of the undocumented, there are the cases of many workers who left families with many children in their country of origin, to return as soon as they make their fortunes, but time passes and soon they establish new families in exile with another such a large number of children, creating a social drama that not even they themselves can overcome.

A very unfortunate social scourge for the Latino community is made up of gang members, highly dangerous criminal elements that control the streets of slums, selling drugs, extorting money from small businesses and involved in criminal acts every day, marking their limits with graffiti. That only they know. In the large Central American colony, the so-called: Salvatruchas, most of them Salvadorans, hence their name, are very feared, they are distinguished by their shaved heads, tattoos on their faces and symbology with their fingers. Thousands of them have been deported, but there are thousands more of the new generations born in America.

There are many programs created to reinsert them into the community in community work, but drug traffickers have in them a large network of dealers who are also dedicated to intimidating young men and girls with weapons, recruiting them for criminal tasks, particularly in schools public.

It is not my task as a writer of Hispanic origin, to take all the dirty laundry out of my community and talk about so many negative things, but hiding them and not confronting them properly is worse. The church, hiding the pedophilia of the high prelates, has done the worst evil, it has only managed to get a multitude of faithful to renounce their faith as charcoal burners and seek shelter in other more reliable religions.

Another of the fields in which the Latino community has stood out has been sports, baseball players, boxers, runners, soccer players have surpassed themselves when it comes to sports contests and have left the so-called bronze race very high. The same can be said with regard to cinema, television, dance, theater and entertainment.

Hollywood from the beginning received the talented contribution of Latin figures, as hundreds of stars sculpted on the asphalt of its streets say to remember them: Rodolfo Valentino, Lupe Vélez, Leo Carrillo, José Mojica, José Ferrer, Cesar Romero, Anthony Queens, Rita Moreno, Dolores de Rio, Antonio Banderas, John Leguizamo, Edward J. Olmos, Rita Hayward, Jenifer López, Salma Hayek, and Raquel Welch.

In the 1950s, the Latin race brought out a very picturesque character within what many called ridiculousness, and others called genius, a macho type, sophisticated and quarrelsome gallant who appeared on the streets of New York's Latin neighborhoods in the decade of the forties, among the so-called Puerto Rican potorros, with great ability to handle the knife and draw doodles on the faces of their enemies, it was nothing more and nothing less than "El Pachuco", the Mexicans claim a large percentage of their humanity, in the Mexican cinema, the actor Tin Tan, with a dress that distinguished him in the community, felt hat and wide-brimmed pants, wide-brimmed pants, high waist, shiny and innovative leather shoes, long jacket below the knee and with a ostentatious gold chain. With a very novel slang in Spanglish "*Órale bato, no la chingues*". The character was idealized by Luis Valdés, choreographer, actor and director, and who gains prominence with the masterful performance of Edward James Olmos, rescuing him from mediocrity in the film: Zoot Suit.

The Mexicans who are called pochos, were not far behind and their kids brought out through the streets of Los Angeles, ostentatious bulging cars that they called Low Riders, sometime later in a great exhibitionist desire. The gangs proliferated in the Mexican neighborhood and many disorders were presented with deaths, injuries and vandalized businesses, burning small businesses in their own community.

But there was also the Moratorium social protest, justified in the so-called Chicano neighborhoods, motivated by the recruitment of young people for the Vietnam War against their will, such as Los Pantheras Negros, a confrontation group from the black neighborhood of Watts, the Chicanos formed in the neighborhood from East Los Angeles, another group they called Los Brown Berets, to confront police brutality and intolerance by authorities, The Chicano movement joined the Third World Liberationist Group and was very active for several years, with approximately 30,000 members , while police belligerence against minorities continued.

There were several victims in the protests in East Los Angeles, the most notorious was the one that occurred on August 29 and in which Los Angeles Times journalist Rubén Salazar died, he was also the news director of KMEX, a news channel news in Spanish, where I worked for a short time, together with William Restrepo. Other victims that day were Lynn Ward and Ángel Diaz. These disastrous dates for the Latino community greatly discouraged the political tasks of the Chicano Movement "La Raza" which entered a long period of inactivity.

In more recent times, the stellar panorama of Hollywood has been enriched with new and numerous Latin stars, as well as directors, producers and writers specialized in modern cinema, who have walked the red carpet all these years, obtaining several Oscars. It is not necessary to list them, but we are stepping strong in the seventh art.

Los Pachucos

Rubén Salazar died in 1970

IMPACT OF ASIAN MINORITIES IN THE AMERICAN UNION

There is already a unified criterion around the first settlers of the American continent, who arrived through the icy lands of the North, specifically about what is the Bering Strait, that in ancient times a series of lakes froze and allowed the passage Thus, it has been confirmed that large groups of Asians, coming from Siberia, were the first to populate these regions, from Alaska, since Asia and America are separated by the sea, anthropologists have confirmed that the remains found are of the Mongoloid type, approximately about 13,000 years ago, the width of the region is about 1,500 kilometers, many of them populated Canada first and along the east coast, they had their settlements in the region of the great lakes, New York, and little by little they were spreading to the south , it is said of some peoples called Iroquois and later others in the region of the rocky mountains and the area of the Mississippi, called the Sioux. They could have been what they would later call: Native Americans.

Approximately 500 peoples are spoken of, the total of different tribes that shared their lives with buffalo, caribou, bears, wolves and reindeer, the extensive northern regions. Thus, the true pioneers were the Asians in creating these settlements before the conquerors of the different empires. In more recent times, the beginning of the 19th century, Asians have surpassed Latin Americans in growth, some 19 million of different ethnicities and from some 30 countries and some 100 languages. The most numerous have been the Chinese, Hindus, Filipinos, Vietnamese, South Koreans and Japanese. A large majority of them have obtained university degrees.

As minorities they have also suffered from the problems of racism, of course on a smaller scale than Latinos and blacks; It must be taken into account that they have been ethnic groups, less conflictive and in their neighborhoods there have never been popular uprisings, strikes, fires and street problems. In addition, among themselves they have organized vigilance committees. In prisons, Asians are detained far fewer than other minorities and instead are becoming more numerous when it comes to seeking higher education.

The Chinese carried out very arduous tasks in past centuries, in the fields of agriculture and also in the construction of the railways, their neighborhoods have stood out for their architecture, always keeping the same models, with well-kept gardening, in regards to food, the Chinese gourmet, in the same way the Japanese, have had a preference among other ethnic groups.

Hindus have been trickling in and some very wealthy, buying up business in hotels and petrol stations, have also gained wide acceptance for their exotic food. In the sixties with the heyday of The Beatles, they led to the importation of some Gurus and brought us transcendental meditation, the music of Rabbi Shancar, spiritual yoga movements proliferated and the arrival of the noisy and exotic Hare Krihsna groups who invaded with their songs and dances, parks, airports, educational centers, important streets, like nomadic gypsies with a great paraphernalia of incense, saris, fantasy jewelry and costume jewelry.

It is important to clarify that at the end of the twenties, the famous guru, Paramahansa Yogananda, settled in Los Angeles, founding his temple in the middle of Sunset Boulevard, in Hollywood, with his evangelizing task of Self Realization, achieving thousands of followers for his cause. Spiritual. As an important fact decades later, the famous teacher also called "The Divine", invited the crowds to witness after some meditations his own death, which occurred to the stupor of a large crowd, for natural reasons.

Years later, another great Master settled in Ojai, California: Jiddu Krishnamurti, promoting the great awakening to a cosmic dimension, whom I had the privilege of meeting together with Master Rene Rebetez, at his study and convention center in the decade the 70s.

Today the Hindu community is very proud to have Kamala Harris, of

Indu descent, as Vice President of the Republic, the first minority woman to reach such a lofty position. A fact of great importance for all minorities is: the universal declaration on cultural diversity, promulgated by UNESCO in October 2021, which gives full recognition to their extraordinary contribution to the aggrandizement of all nations.

Bruce Lee: Asian Movie Star

Korean mother fleeing from fallen Seoul, 1951

Asian women like Latinas work and they attend to household chores at the same time.

A NUMEROUS ETHNIC GROUP WITHOUT NAME AND DISTINCTIVES

In the United States there is a large resident community of different races that lives with the others without caring about what happens in the system, particularly alien to political currents, of a vegetative and superlatively conformist type, accepts all changes without protesting, is not interested in It's a damn who's in charge and much less which party, in political matters they don't see, they don't hear and they don't understand, it doesn't matter to them and it's a great majority, and they enjoy the system, consume and live a normal life, work, pay pays taxes, goes to church, prays, gives alms, listens to the pastors, celebrates its festivals, fills the stadiums and entertainment venues, is very participative, sees everything normal, does not attend protests, strikes or demonstrations.

Some call them conformists, the lukewarm, and indifferent. They do not vote for any candidate and they agree with those who win, they do not care what tendency they are, or what their government program is, including many housewives, ladies in hats, loving mothers, fiery lovers, golf players, anonymous alcoholics, television viewers and patrons of casinos and bars. Thanks to these people, the candidates are chosen by a Democratic or Republican minority. For these lukewarm or indifferent whoever wins, everything will be the same, things are fine as they are, as long as their interests are not spoiled.

In the statistics they are one more piece of the living conglomerate and the elites agree with their conduct or proceeding, because it is not harmful or conflictive. In almost all societies in the world they exist, they are called masses or non-participatory populism, The Silent Mayorit (The Silent Majority). There are many rulers who have come to power with votes of less than 50% and losing the popular vote, four of them Republicans. In a democratic society with so many guarantees to elect, this is not acceptable, with so many millions that the parties spend on advertising for their candidates and all that their conventions cost. For this reason, we will be condemned to be governed by a minority due to the absence of voters in the elections. Corruption and unfulfilled promises are also reasons for desertion and voter fatigue.

THE LONG AND PROLONGED STRUGGLE OF WOMEN FOR CONQUERING YOUR RIGHTS

As in almost all the countries of the world, women have had to fight openly to win their rights; There are very few countries that have granted them spontaneously and without having to fight great battles, even for the most elementary ones to be recognized, such as equality before men.

North America has been no exception. Since the time of the revolution to get rid of the tutelage of England, although many guarantees had already been given, it took a long time to implement them and make them effective.

The native women of the various communities also lived in disadvantaged situations, subjugated by men and with a number of responsibilities that included working in the fields and in the house, plus the care of the children absorbed most of their time, this did not It is nothing new, since time immemorial according to the biblical texts, Eve had already been condemned to the worst tasks due to original sin; stories and legends aside, the reality is that almost everywhere the role of women has always been overburdened with domestic obligations in savage and civilized societies.

Frances Perkins was a student who, before obtaining academic degrees, was a pioneer of social struggles in America, as was Mary McLeod, a black educator who had long fought for the rights of minorities with the advice of Eleanor Roosevelt. During the 1930s Great Depression, some 400,000 people of Mexican American descent were deported, despite being legal residents or born in America.

Machismo has become the worst scourge to keep women in inferior conditions and this phenomenon is present in almost all parts of the globe: Asia, Africa, Europe and Latin America, the American Union has not been the exception, something very frequent in minority neighborhoods.

Sex has been the only weapon to achieve man's privileges and be able to enslave him. The conception of equalities, many times has been worse, not for her benefit, but quite the opposite in making her responsible with jobs that were previously destined for men, in terms of what has been called: Women's liberation, many times it is a kind of trap into which she has fallen, trying to take advantage, she has renounced what for a long time was considered courtesies towards the weaker sex, giving them a seat in transportation, making small conceptions for them, opening the car door or that they did not have to share the account in invitations to the theater or the restaurant.

With regard to fashion, the French couturier Yves Saint Laurel, a student of Christian Dior, was one of those who contributed the most to the idea that women wear masculine clothes, he put elegant feminine clothes in vogue, almost equal to that of men. Older women found men's pants very comfortable and dressers and coordinated it with very short haircuts, which looking from behind, seemed true macho. But that is not the end of what the woman sought with her liberation was to demonstrate that she could also do the same tasks, which were entrusted to men due to their rudeness and indelicacy for female hands. Then the female faces appeared at the wheel of tractor-mules, in foundry workshops, mechanics, building construction and even managing banks, hotels, driving planes, ships and even war tanks.

Overalls-type Blue Jeans were adopted as one of the daily garments for women and combined with blouses and even became universal for men, women, the elderly and children. Like chewing gum, cigarettes and potato chips are all over the globe in homes, men with aprons began to be seen doing housework and taking care of children, cooking, washing dishes and cleaning routines.

Women's liberation also led them to give up one of their best qualities such as delicacy, trying to be like men and wanting to equal them, they adopted one of the worst male clothing, rustic overalls with suspenders, haircut, rudeness in work and manners, rude and foul language and wanting to do the worst jobs that require excess strength and energy.

The so-called feminism in women has been disappearing, silk in dresses, overalls and blue jeans, few women no longer smell of perfumes, but men's deodorant. High-heeled shoes have been replaced by rough work or tennis shoes, this has allowed mistakes to be made when believing who is a man or a woman in a social gathering. Returning to the main theme of the struggle of women for their most basic rights in the United States, it has been very bloody and even fierce in its early stages, when it received police brutality and was frequently imprisoned in its street protests. Regarding the treatment they receive in workshops, factories, fields or work in restaurants, hotels, hospitals, women always had the worst part, when foremen and bosses abused their status as second-class people, wages were least for women, even though they had the same responsibilities as men.

Speaking of dates, the great battle of women for the right to vote began in 1840, when a real interest in organizing was born, taking advantage of a great campaign that was taking place against alcoholic beverages and its consequences within the family, history texts mention Elizabeth Cady Stanton as one of the first leaders of feminism, along with Lucrecia Mott at the Convention in Seneca Falls, New York in 1848. Years later, in 1869, the National Association of Women for Feminism was created. suffrage (National Woman Suffrage Association) where another leader Lucy Stone, also an activist in the anti-slavery struggle, stands out, calling for the right to vote without taking into account racial status. This movement was joined by religious groups, who saw slavery as degrading and a great sin in the eyes of God. The association was made up of working middle-class women and radicals as well. Many of them reached the grounds of the White House, for which a large majority were imprisoned despite the absence of violence in these protests. When they resorted to Hunger Strikes, the unions gained new supporters for their cause.

Several legislator politicians joined the meetings with eloquent speeches and it was also the time of the First World War, in which women played an important role in all the rough and delicate jobs, also in hospitals and other children's centers. Flora Tristan, a recognized socialist leader, played an important role in the fight for women's rights, as did Betty Freedman years later. In France, Simone Beauvoir was a fighter for the rights of women, wife of Jean Paul Sartre, in her work: The Second Sex, she makes her revolutionary thinking felt.

Despite the fact that a large consensus of supporters of the female vote was already national, it had to take a long time for its approval with an amendment and that required state legislation to become official on August 18, 1920. But it is important to understand that the achievement of the right to suffrage also cost a lot in humiliation, imprisonment and mistreatment, that the leaders suffered from the terror of the authorities of that time, who did not give a truce to women who had to share the hours of rest to be able to attend the commitments with the fight for suffrage. Eleanor Roosevelt, wife of the 32nd president of the United States, was one of the first women to stand out nationally and internationally as a leader of social work for the emancipation of women's rights, traveling throughout the country and creating a new awareness of overcoming in a time as difficult as the 1940s were in the 20th century. At the most crucial time of the black struggle for civil rights, a humble woman named Rosa Parks, developed a campaign that inspired the creation of SCLC, when she refused to give up her seat on the bus to a white man who was pressuring her threateningly. In 1955 in Montgomery.

Regarding the religious part, this has become a powerful obstacle to the advancement of women, they have opposed their rights to abortion, use of condoms, to women holding an important position in the clergy and the have always relegated to the background. In the United States, it must be recognized that the new legislation has greatly favored women, particularly since the beginning of the 21st century, their participation in managerial positions in the government and private companies has been very notorious. We have had a woman candidate for the presidency: Hillary Clinton and now we have Kamala Harris as vice president, in addition to several senators, one of the most prominent being Nancy Pelosi.

The achievement obtained by women in birth control has been very important, Margaret Higgins Sanger, a woman nurse and also leader of a women's movement, worked in the last stages of her life in the 90s of the last centuries with poor women, because they adopted contraceptive methods in search of avoiding abortions later due to economic problems, she also founded a newspaper The Woman Rebel, and for her campaigns she was imprisoned several times. Birth control had a very important boom in the

United States, advising couples to have only two, to avoid the Overpopulation Bomb, which its author Paul Ehrlich referred to in 1968.

A pillar of feminism and liberation in the 1960s, Hellen Gurley Brown, author of the book: The Sex and the single girl. Creator of a prototype of an independent, hard-working, demanding, idealistic woman and not very fond of marriage or ties, she hated the term weaker sex, unconcerned about motherhood, her ideology was to be free. Editor of Cosmopolitan magazine, where her mission was to illustrate and recommend the best for modern women.

The Arab nations and with the Muslim religion in between, are the ones that have put up a lot of resistance in granting women the most basic rights, countries where they live in secular backwardness and a large number of nations on the African continent, where it seems inconceivable that in the age of the conquest of the cosmos and space travel, women in these countries live as if they were in the age of caves. In the stone age women were almost naked with some tail cover, now the orthodox Arabs force them to be very covered from head to toe, with a small girdle that barely allows them to see turmas in several Asian countries and many on the African continent. Women live in very disadvantaged conditions and carry many responsibilities at home and at work. Something similar can be seen in Latin America, particularly in farm work, where they carry their children while they are working.

A criminal act that is repeated every day, at least in thirty countries, and especially in the so-called Black Continent with minor girls, is related to their sexual life and they are forced to have a cut in their vagina to practically remove their clitoris sold by their parents before reaching puberty.

Feminism had its greatest preponderance in America in the 60s and 70s, in which it developed a great agitation, as a participant in strikes and social movements for their rights and against the Vietnam War, active in what was the Hippie Community, Gloria Steiner in these decades stood out as a fiery leader, writer, from Ohio and of Jewish origin, founder of an MS MAGAZINE publication dedicated as a spokesperson for the feminist cause to raise awareness and promote substantial changes and human rights reforms and civil unrecognized women; she soon became iconic as a feminist counselor. Similarly, the actress Jane Fonda traveled to Vietnam in the middle of the war in favor of stopping the conflict and the genocide of so many victims and awakening a new national consciousness, daughter of another great actor Henry Fonda.

Feminism in its initial moment, was a worldwide phenomenon, which encouraged to end the repression of so much injustice for women's rights and achieved many advances that could not have been made a reality, without the support of the new organizations in gestation.

For Latin America it was a great example, as political leaders emerged who have held administrative positions in the government and in private companies. Long before in the American Union, women have distinguished themselves in politics, Eva Perón in Argentina, María Cano in Colombia, Su Frida Kahlo in Mexico, Manuela Sanz in Ecuador and in recent years, Violeta Chamorro in Nicaragua, Michelle Bachelet in Chile, and Mireya Moscoso in Panama. Dilma Rousseff in Brazil and Cristina Kirchner in Argentina.

Gloria Steiner : organizer of the Feminist Movement.

Woman facing the American military force

THE WALL: THE TORTILLAS CURTAIN

"Between your house and my house there is a wall of silence. A wall so that the people can never jump over it".

Raphael de Leon.

This is a drama that has been increasing alarmingly in recent years and that has taken North America by surprise, numerous undocumented immigrants, knocking hard on doors, desperately waiting for their immigration papers to be initiated, and at the same time for their immigration papers to be resolved problems of housing, food and health services, with the family that accompanies them, at the foot of the retaining wall, to southern California and Texas while other large groups are on their way. Donald Trump in 2018, enemy of minorities, began to rebuild an existing wall with the purpose of making it as impassable as possible, justifying his action with the criterion that it is to prevent the entry of criminals.

In this case it is also worth establishing responsibilities with the country of origin, where they come from; granting exit papers, passports without a visa to the country where they are heading, allowing entry to the nations that are in transit and more if they are crowds in unsanitary conditions. Mexico, as a border nation where this exodus of families is headed, has to overcome the greatest responsibility, to give them protection, housing and food during the period that the waiting period lasts, at the foot of the wall, in addition to ensuring their safety as well, as they are vulnerable to crime.

"This damn wall"

Popular folklore.

Outside of the Great Wall of China, so extensive, today almost a museum piece, there are very few that exist in the world, impassable to separate borders; that of the United States, erected with a high cost from coast to coast, from west to east and for which Donald Trump demanded that Mexico pay half the value, is now unfinished. The wall has become a subject with many contradictions, every nation has the right to protect its borders, since organized crime uses it to pass contraband, drugs and weapons, extorting many undocumented immigrants as drug mules.

The wall that has always existed has many flaws, due to its extension in many parts, it has areas that are difficult to build and its cost is very high, Trump left it unfinished. Another problem is the proliferating underground tunnels through which thousands of undocumented immigrants enter, plus the smuggling of weapons, drugs, liquor and merchandise without paying taxes.

With the limits to the north, the border with Canada, there are no major problems, although each nation has its own responsibilities and the problems that exist in the south do not arise.

Mexico is not very interested in this problem, because in a certain way it benefits from the exodus of its overpopulation, and it seeks to go into exile, which is increasing, and if they go north, they will receive more dollars with the remittances they send to their relatives, the who go looking for work.

When the Berlin Wall existed, in East Germany during the dictatorship of Walther Ulbricht, a great believer in the communist cause, this wall was tall and made of concrete with barbed wire and watchtowers like the one in prisons. Many were the victims who succumbed trying to escape to the allied sector, that's why it was called The Wall of Infamy,

At the end of World War II, the United States took advantage of this situation to make its political propaganda condemning the idea of separating borders with walls. Jack Kennedy condemned the violence that occurred with guards shooting at those who wanted to flee west, fleeing the communist authoritarian system. The wall was demolished by volunteers from both sectors, and many families that were separated, came together again in a brotherly embrace, Kennedy never thought of similar problems in North America, of course, today's situations are different with the wall that exists in this to the west, border with Mexico, now they fight to enter, while in communist Germany it was to leave.

The Rio Grande or Rio Bravo, have been the main limits on the border with Mexico, its geographical location in the vicinity of the southern part, makes it easy for many to swim across, but the water flow is very treacherous and many have lost their lives in the attempt, those who make it through are contemptuously called: wet (Mojados).

The steel wall, programmed by D. Trump for those who seek a paradise.

Berlin Wall

SELLING PARADISE

"Pass my black, it happens that the road is carpeted".

Cuban folklore.

There are numerous people around the world who would like to live in the United States, since this nation became a great power, the economy is one factor, the facilities to obtain benefits is another, to acquire education, work and enjoy comfort, the existing technology like other powers, and the high standard of living, which make many underdeveloped nations envy it. Although its democracy is not perfect, many nations live in worse circumstances, continuous, authoritarian, corrupt and criminal dictatorships. That is why the idea of paradise arose, which for many can now turn out to be just a nightmare.

Far from being so, there are also many problems such as racism, inversion of values, intolerance and corruption, in some cities, ghettos in neighborhoods with gangs and overcrowding in streets with housing problems. For these groups of Central Americans who are looking for a paradise to live in, this no longer exists, they arrived late, the panorama that is seen now is not very encouraging in cities like Los Angeles, to arrange immigration papers, these can take up to ten years as undocumented person. The best thing is to stay in your country, even if it means enduring needs with your own, with your language, with your customs, with your own race, but that is if you fight to improve yourself and try to change bad things, not be an accomplice of corruption.

A lot of that American paradise is fantasy, too, that money is on the ground, that jobs are easy, that a month after you arrive you already have a car, that rich blondes are looking for Latino males, that a year later you already have a house for the family and that the American state is going to provide you with everything you need while you get a job, that the English language is easy and you can speak it a month after you arrive, and that you can buy the resident visa around the corner corner. Countryman, wake up from the enchantment, they don't give as much good stuff.

The Capitalist System that operates in the United States is not a world charity organization, although on many occasions it is very generous, as in the case of a catastrophe or a tsunami. The system has been created by the owners of capital, to create wealth and take advantage of opportunities to increase it, it is not a totalitarian system and at the same time it is the complete opposite of socialism. Of course, the system has been changing since its inception and is no longer what Karl Marx fought against in 1880, with his work: Capital.

At that time, working hours were 14 hours, from Monday to Saturday, there were no holidays, vacations or sick pay, and the workshops and workspaces lacked security and protection systems against accidents, wages were 25 cents. At the time, deaths were very frequent and there were no compensations. Reasons enough for a protest against such injustice to have prospered

The importance of the Hegelian Dialectic is also widely recognized and its system was created by the German philosopher George Hegel, who theorized that the center of the universe is an absolute spirit, which guides all realities. The third law of his dialectic is the pendulum theory. The extreme faces are called Thesis, antithesis and its resolution are the synthesis, based on this explanation, it is understood that Hegel was right that human beings can understand the unfolding of history.

North America has many things of Socialism: social security, which although it is not perfect, works, an unemployment system that covers the needs in the event of being laid off, or becoming disabled. A retirement system for those who reached the age of majority and paid their taxes during the regulatory period. A medical care and hospitalization service. A service for Welfare care homes, when they have been neglected by the husband. A free educational program for children's early and secondary education. There are many more benefits that other countries with a capitalist system do not offer, although many do not want to understand this is socialism, even if they do not like the term.

It is obvious that like any political system, not everything works perfectly, there are flaws, corruption, but things go on despite the difficulties. The Political Party for which you vote has a great responsibility in the performance of its duties.

Of course, this capitalist society knows how to sell itself, for that it has media such as cinema, radio and television recreating paradises with all the comfort that is why you must be aware, so that this dream does not turn into a nightmare.

One of the pillars of Capitalism, was a Scottish economist Adam Smith, 1723 - 1790, with very conservative ideas expressed in his work: "The Wealth of Nations", "Money Game", in which he supported a capitalist accumulation thought based on in marketing, to free competition, to the development of production and to limit the government in its interventions.

Smith was a brilliant expositor of his ideas, a professor at the University of Glasgow, and the one who proposed a market system: Laissez - Faire Marquet. Another outstanding capitalist theory was the Englishman David Ricardo, a Sephardic Jew of Portuguese descent, a follower of Adam Smith's theses, who amassed a respectable fortune with his free trade businesses.

John Maynard Keyes was another great English economist who promoted the capitalist system.

Capitalism, throughout its history, has had great successes, but also its great setbacks and spectacular falls. In North America, the most disastrous was the one from 1929 to 1933, which had a great global impact, but after the Second World War it managed to recover, during the administration of Franklin Delano Roosevelt. Before and after it had other crises, but not so spectacular, important factors in these falls have been: overproduction, price fluctuations, exports and imports, lack of markets, lack of liquidity, under consumption and fictitious capital. Today it has two major supports, the International Monetary Fund and the World Bank, but there are also another series of drawbacks due to its dependence on computers that are sometimes interrupted by the action of hackers, a kind of bandits in the systems. Also, a prolonged blackout for several days can create an economic crisis.

It was the year 1883, the capitalist system operated with a series of ups and downs and several organizations, unions or trade unions, with memberships in the working classes, worked, one of the first was called: The Knights of Labor Knights of Labor that had great support, its president was a machinist Terence Powderly, who at the time was presenting a List of Petitions in which they asked for the approval of several measures: an eight-hour work schedule, equal opportunities for women and a prohibition of work for children under 14.

These petitions were implementing a series of strikes, one of which had the greatest attendance was the one that took place on May 1, 1886, in a Chicago market place, Haymarket Square, with an approximate number of two thousand attendees.

The explosion of a bomb that occurred suddenly left approximately 30 dead and 1200 wounded, it is said that a group of anarchist assistants, the terrorists of the time, were responsible. Sacco and Vanzetti were convicted and sentenced to death, although the evidence was never found. On May 1 of each year, it is commemorated as the holiday of work, to remember this disastrous date of 1886, for all the workers of the world as the Chicago massacre, with marches and massive acts. Only the United States does not give credit to this commemoration and has chosen another date in the month of September to remember Labor Day.

Women working in factories 1920.

Illustration about the Haymarket massacre in Chicago (1886).

ECONOMIC TERRORISM

Economic terrorism can be considered almost as deadly as a large-scale military incursion, except that it is silent, and for many it goes unnoticed and does not produce an immediate reaction. It can only be activated by those who manage the powerful economies, such as the so-called great powers, and who can militarily support any intention to circumvent them. This terrorism also works on a smaller scale, like the one applied by banking or credit entities with a company that does not accept their tax rates.

During Obama's presidential period, "The Real Estate Bubble" was presented, banking entities associated with real estate companies fictitiously created a great economic disaster and then requested a financial rescue from the government, which was granted to them. A vast majority of middle-class families lost their homes due to high interest rates, life savings and practically stripped of what they thought they had a home.

The bubble occurs due to an excessive increase in the value of real estate or real estate for speculative purposes, based on supply and demand, but it suddenly explodes and the entire inflated system collapses, to return to real prices, which the winners are those who propitiated it and those who lose, those who lent themselves to the game.

An extortion that occurs day by day, is applied by managers, foremen, and senior executives of the official bureaucracy or of private companies with the employees and threatening them to leave them vacant or accept sexual favors in exchange. A kind of Right of Pernada. This is a widespread problem all over the world.

In its time Russia also applied it with the countries of the Union of Soviet Socialist Republics, particularly in the Stalinist era. Great Britain imposed it on India, which was its colony until 1948, when M. Gandhi obtained its liberation.

In practice, economic terrorism is to corner a country, surround it in its economic needs, and prevent other nations from helping it with extortion, until it is subdued, in some cases, many do not see it but as a forced measure. Putin is doing something similar with Ukraine.

In Equatorial Africa many soldiers use it for lack of weapons and the result is prolonged famines, where the victims are children, women and the elderly.

The overseas powers resorted to these methods. Spain besieged Cartagena de India's due to hunger: Colombia, during the time of Independence, which succumbed before surrendering. In the 21st century, there is talk of free trade agreements that are constantly changing and are applied like chess practiced by the great powers.

Venezuela has managed to evade economic restrictions, thanks to the corruption that operates on a large scale and its oil wealth, operated by a military clique, where a dance of millions operates. A large majority of the people have adopted the exodus, considered 30 percent, forced across all their borders; even the most ardent anti-Chavistas have abandoned the fight, despite Nicolas Maduro's generous promise to retire in the 2050s, by which time several other military officers are already lining up.

In other terms to which the word terrorism is no longer applied is: To be under the influence of a conditional friendship of exchange, such as that practiced by many Latin American nations with the United States, China with its neighboring countries, or those that already they are indebted to him, Russia with its former Soviet nations maintains a policy of submission or friendship and others of a threatening nature to invade it.

In the middle of the last century, under the patronage of the United States, the Organization of American States, O.E.A., was created. headquartered in Washington, after the failed Pan-American Union, a way to control the backyard, at that time the Department of State, was fortunate to use the unconditional services of a Colombian citizen named: Alberto Lleras

Camargo, who lent himself to convince all the countries of Latin America to enter the ring, of course he was the first Secretary, with payment in dollars and a large series of perks and privileges.

The idea was not bad at all, it was about the union of Latin American nations jointly facing all the existing problems, underdevelopment, unemployment, land ownership, the problem of anti-democratic dictatorships, feudalism and others, of course their Meetings were in the presence of the master or his representative and in his own home, Washington, where the headquarters or General Directorate operates.

For this reason, the OAS has distinguished itself by its ineffectiveness, as they say over there "A lot of dicks, dick and few palettes." Since they keep us so divided with Cain behavior, the organization has not been able to prosper.

"In God we trust", a message on American bills and coins.

THE PUBLIC PROBLEM OF DRUG TRAFFICKING

"I bring yerba santa for the throat."

Cuban folklore.

The United States as a great economic power, which they look at and admire a lot for its free trade, has been invaded by numerous criminal mafias, which operate controlled by the forces of order and others uncontrolled by the existing corruption, this is nothing new, it comes Centuries ago, when the American Union generously opened the doors to a migration that came from all over the world, but at that time there were no controls and criminals entered with their families to establish their modus operandi, gangsters and bandits that they found in the twenties of the last century a fertile territory, with unemployment, overcrowding, the variety of races, the proliferation of dangerous suburbs and the lack of surveillance. Irish and Italians were the pioneers in crime, particularly in the big cities, Chicago, New York, San Francisco, Detroit and others. La Camorra, La Mano Negra, Cosa Nostra began their criminal career with extortion, gambling, and alcoholic beverages (prohibited at the time).

In view of the lucrative market that the so-called heroic drugs represent all over the world, the mafias have used this rich territory of the USA to buy and sell wholesale and retail their stocks of all kinds of narcotics such as amazing cocaine and heroin. and opioids that arrive at its headquarters every day from different parts of the world on yachts, submarines, planes and through the many tunnels south of the border to satisfy the demand of celebrity luminaries and the entertainment of some sportsmen and tycoons of private companies and why not, also of the chilling world of the underworld. The most dangerous ones because they create a dependency are the chemical ones, like crack and on the market, they are the cheapest. White slavery, prostitution, extortion, money laundering and the illegal sale of weapons are added to this market.

Thanks to their wealth and tolerance, in the American union there are many addicts who pay high prices and keep the opioid market active, movie luminaries, entertainment stars and millionaire sports, all have a candle at this funeral.

During his visit to Colombia, General Norman Schwarzkopf, who commanded US troops in the invasion of Iraq to expel Saddam Hussein from Kuwait in 1996, was interviewed by Semana magazine about the problem of drug trafficking and the international struggle to eradicate it, he said:

'Drug trafficking is a monster with four heads: the production process, trafficking from producer countries to consumer countries, distribution in consumer countries and consumption, despite the efforts, I believe that my country has not done enough that it should do, the problem is that the more it is attacked, the supply with an intact demand the prices tend to rise. Another theoretical solution would be the legalization of drugs, because that would put an end to the business of crime, of course there are also serious moral and public health implications that cannot be ignored'.

These ideas are the same that I supported in my book "EXCELSO Y AMARGO" long ago, when the government-controlled production by legalizing it, but this does not mean that it recommends the state to plant, it would simply take the business away from crime, decriminalizing it with a reasonable price to the addicts of the stocks they have which they continually confiscate and helping them to end their dependency as has happened with liquors, tobacco, marijuana.

A large part of the national budget is used to try to control this varied scourge with powerful technology that now also includes space satellites to control routes and drones with weapons and tracking cameras. Although the amount that is confiscated every day by the authorities is considerable, the enormous profits that the mafias receive are enough not to be discouraged and continue their criminal task; the victims are part and part.

The United States not only spends on the control of its borders, but also on economic aid to other countries, to destroy cocaine and heroin crops, with regard to marijuana, now this has been considered less harmful and is being legalized by all parts and allowing its cultivation on a smaller scale, but all this is taxable, pays tax.

Although the United States is considered the richest market in the world, also because of its growing dependence, it is the nation that has the luxury of certifying nations that have drug dependency such as Colombia. The guerrillas and the paramilitaries no longer seek political control, now they fight each other for the best drug trafficking routes.

The saddest part is that their coca production is consumed by a growing number of new addicts in Colombia itself. As long as the price of cocaine is higher than that of coffee, the main product for which he receives his foreign exchange, the crops will continue and there is a lot of territory of large forests, where they can hide. The areas that are fumigated suffer a lot from the chemicals and require expensive treatments to re-enable them to other crops. When the three most important drug cartels disappeared, the mini-cartels emerged, the problem atomized. Every time the government seizes tons of cocaine, the price goes up. In exchange for fighting the market, the authorities should establish a market for it and sell it, at reasonable prices, through licenses, as is being done with marijuana, in this way organized crime would not obtain the enormous sums it receives, in the so-called black market.

The United States has already had this problem with alcohol of prohibiting it and taking it away from the mafias as in the decades of the 20s, the famous era of Alcapone, legalizing it and obtaining profits from it and creating centers to end dependency. Alcoholics Anonymous.

In the middle of the 1800 century there was a movement called "Temperance", a society that sought to prohibit the consumption and production of alcoholic beverages as they were considered harmful to health and degrading to American families; it spread to almost every other state in the union and most women backed the campaign unifying it in pursuit of the right to vote, calling it the Women's Christian League (WCTU) Anti-Salon League in 1895. To getting legislative bodies to support them, President Woodrow Wilson himself backed the measures. Its greatest success was to get it ratified as an amendment to the constitution in 1778, confirming the prohibition of producing, selling and consuming alcoholic beverages throughout the territory for seven years.

These measures made the company more interesting and adventurous, which is why (Bootleggers) emerged, who took advantage of the night hours to distill intoxicating drinks with great profits, which caused them to proliferate everywhere, as small companies and even in neighboring nations such as Mexico and Canada in great demand. Organized crime took over such a flourishing and lucrative market, becoming a true epidemic, which forced the authorities to modify the Amendments on February 20, 1933, legalizing alcohol, after having it prohibited for 13 years, to which W Wilson had called him, A noble experiment. Since then, the government has taken control of the beverages, ended the criminal industry and market, but also obtained a source of profit for the nation.

Mafia-run slot machines that the government seized in frequent raids were legalized and now function in big casinos like Las Vegas. Tobacco and cigarettes were previously prohibited, now legalized but with great control with great campaigns to end their dependence.

UNITED STATES AND THE UNITED NATIONS

This world organization was born as the League of Nations, when the Treaty of Versailles was created, at the end of the First World War (1914 to 1918) with the absence of the United States, which refused to ratify it despite the fact that Woodrow Wilson did so. Had presented as one of his personal initiatives, to solve the constant problems of the world.

The League's main purpose was to try to find a solution to the imperialist interventions of Italy with Ethiopia, Japan in Manchuria and Germany with Austria. Although its efforts were ineffective and practically constituted the reason for its dissolution, but during the time of World War II, the foundations were laid for what was later reborn as the United Nations, with its headquarters in New York. The League of Nations dissolved itself during the time of World War II 1939 -1945.

Because the headquarters of the organization is in the territory of the United States, the leaders of the affiliated nations present themselves to render their reports, every time they are summoned, the Security Council works there in the same building, which has the responsibility to consider the problems that arise, when world peace is in danger.

In the sixties, of the last century, characters like Ernesto Che Guevara and Fidel Castro and the Venezuelan Hugo Chávez, made their speeches, Castro spoke for six hours, his grievances memorial, other unpleasant characters for the State Department, and they have the opportunity to vent their complaints and tantrums before other attending leaders.

It is the United Nations agency that is concerned with the most critical problems of the globe, its directors make the appropriate suggestions and take the measures on what actions should be taken to solve them. Some powers go ahead and make decisions unilaterally, that only the U.N. correspond, according to their interests.

By 2007 it already had 192 affiliated nations, of the first 51 originally registered, with six groups in different tasks and the one with the greatest responsibility is security, the Security Council as a preserver of peace, others for the field of economy and also to rule justice.

THE EXPERIENCES DO NOT SERVE BUT TO FALL INTO THE SAME ERRORS

Those Who Do Not Remember the Past

Are Commanded to Repeat it.

Someone out there coined this phrase that is very interesting to apply to the repeated behavior of North American politics, which has been taken as a corollary of most of its wrong acts, by different Republican and Democratic administrations.

Since those responsible for these acts of arbitrariness do not receive the punishment they deserve, even though they have a press and media to denounce them, these are no more than embarrassing acts that the community finds out about and in the end accepts them with indifference, as part of the political game that is why they are repeated.

The school massacres that are already more than twenty, fill the community with stupor, everyone beats their chests, but the astonishment soon ends, until they appear again. Children wielding sophisticated assault weapons, which parents buy and keep in their cupboards without worrying. In some homes there are real arsenals, which can be obtained easily, as promotional bargains. To obtain them there is no prior criminal investigation, it is enough to have a driver's license, you can also order them by mail.

But these acts that happen at home, are of minor importance, they are soon forgotten. Those caused by the leaders in the other White House, are more serious and among them the faults are forgiven and become part of history. Wars with millions of victims and exorbitant costs that could have been avoided like the one in Vietnam and which its managers shamefully had to recognize as mistakes.

The same thing happened with Cuba, if a government like that of Fulgencio Batista had not been allowed to turn Havana into a brothel in the Caribbean, with economic aid and weapons from the United States, and that criminal mafias would operate, Fidel Castro's revolution could not have prospered.

Likewise, if the State Department had not allowed a North American company: United Fruit Company, to mercilessly exploit several Central American countries, try to appoint presidents like Castillo Armas in Guatemala and overthrow legally constituted leaders like Jacobo Árbenz, a war would not have happened. With so many victims. Mama Yunai, had previously caused a great massacre of humble peasants in banana plantations for not paying a simple and fair salary increase in Colombia, years ago denounced by Jorge Eliecer Gaitán and literally recreated by the Nobel Prize winner, García Márquez in his work One Hundred Years of Solitude.

If the United States had not helped with money and weapons to perpetuate a score of satraps and dictators for fear of communism such as: Somoza, Batista, Trujillo, Pérez Jiménez, Castillo Armas, Stroessner, Odría, Videla, Duvalier, Noriega, Rojas Pinilla and others outside the American continent; another would be the panorama with another type of less macabre and terrorist policy and with less expensive and more generous and humanist programs.

Many of the great mistakes of North America, which have cost it multimillion-dollar figures and have damaged the prestige earned by other noble causes, have been carried out silently, using Machiavellian and criminal intelligence like Kissinger's in previous decades. Fearsome criminal commitments have been hidden from the American people by many presidents for fear of losing votes in a presidential re-election.

How long will North American society continue to turn a blind eye to such repeated mistakes? This is also a form of acceptance of everything that the political elite do and it is nothing more than the product of a sick Society, already in a state of prostration. As the rector of mercantilist capitalism and a world power, other nations closely follow its conduct: If they do it, why can't we do it too?

The United States is the image of what is repeated in other places, its fashions, its scandals, the cinema and television are in charge of spreading what should be done: fast food, torn and faded blue jeans, little ethics, a very below the limits, dehumanized and with a great crisis of behavior in the homes and a future with many questions: where is this alienated society headed, sick repeating its same mistakes of violence, intolerance, warmongering, ostentation, racism, supremacy , armament and pretending to be the perfect society, the paradise of the world, to which we must pay homage?

In my opinion, the modern powers must be democratized and directed under other humanist premises, to help underdeveloped countries overcome the existing problems of overpopulation, better use of technical machinery in agriculture, forget the arms race, end corruption, live democratically with free elections, not allowing re-election or continuity, making substantial reforms in the economy and applying justice with equity. Simply by applying these formulas, we would arrive at an acceptable degree of modern ideal democracy.

United Fruit Company advertisement for bananas.

Fast foods are the most popular food among Americans.

THE DARK SIDE OF PARADISE

In the XXI century there are many migrants who seek to reside in the United States from all over the world, thanks to the existing economic level and the image of well-being that it projects through the media, also to the large uninhabited extensions that it has, despite the Candidates for new residents will have to face a series of obstacles, obstacles and commitments, which reduce the enthusiasm and joy with which they came, after crossing the threshold of the immigration offices. Paradise has many demons and after you wake up from your dream, it will not be in Disneyland, you will have to face a new experience.

North America has forgotten to publicly clarify the true reality that its paradise represents, to do so would avoid many problems, especially with the unwanted ones whose goal is to establish themselves at any cost. Also, with those who have forged a wrong idea of what the northern country is, deluded with the notion of making millions in a short time, of finding work without having a profession, of starting to send dollars to their country of origin every week of having arrived, speaking English in a short time and pretending to circumvent the laws as they are used to, driving without a license and sometimes drunk. Dollars are elusive and painstakingly earned, learn to daydream.

THE CHILLING ARTIFICIAL PARADISE OF THE AMAZING

In the long-awaited American Union in which many would like to live and cannot, there is another paradise that is enjoyed every day by movie luminaries, Olympic athletes, celebrity and entertainment artists, a large number of addicts, a growing youth in schools, colleges and universities, to these groups we must add the most criminal, the underworld that enjoys and lives from its market, I am referring to the artificial paradise of hallucinogens and intoxicating drugs.

A powerful industry that moves millions, allied with others such as prostitution, white slavery, smuggling, money laundering, extortion and organized crime with large international contacts and to which cocaine, heroin, and marijuana arrive through different channels opium; to these we must add those that are easily manufactured at home, such as crack.

Although it must be recognized that the government has a sophisticated army to repress it and spends enormous amounts of the budget to deal with this crime, the statistics continue to show the enormous profits they obtain and the number of victims they cause.

The United States is the most preferred market for mind-blowing drugs, not only because of the price of its currency, enormous extensions that it possesses, which lend themselves to their arrival and make surveillance difficult; the tolerance of its neighboring nations, it must also be considered that there is a lot of corruption that favors operations.

She was showing him her belly button ring when she frowned and pinched a bit of skin from around her belly.

“Do you think I’m fat?” She asked, suddenly.

He laughed.

“Not at all.”

“It’s too bad we can’t play some music.” She said. “I haven’t danced in a long time. Ever since the injury. But I’m getting stronger.”

She fell forward on his lap.

“Whoa,” Officer Miley said. “Maybe you should get some rest. I wouldn’t want your parents to walk in on us like this. They might get the wrong idea about me.”

“Oh, they’re not my parents.” Annie said, standing back up.

“Step parents, I meant.” Officer Miley corrected.

“They’re not my step parents either.” She said. “I’m just living here till I get back on my feet, so to speak.”

“Oh,” Officer Miley said. “Well, I wouldn’t want you to over exert yourself.”

“I’m okay. Are you sure you don’t want to dance with me?” Annie asked. “It might help with my insomnia.”

Annie started to dance and sing softly, snapping her fingers, “Go shorty. It’s your birthday. We gonna party like it’s your birthday…” She gave me a wink as officer Miley stood up to dance with her.

I tiptoed passed them as Annie rested her head under his chin and fell against him.

“Careful now.” He said, as he helped steady her on her feet.

I stepped back into my room trying not to make any noise.

As I closed the door, I could hear Annie humming the rest of the song to herself in a dreamlike state.

I got undressed and went to bed in my boxers and a t-shirt.

I slept till almost 5pm.

My mom peeped in a few times to check in on me. That’s what she told me when I finally got up. They had decided to let me sleep in as late as I needed.

I was putting on the same pair of jeans I wore last night when dad stepped into my room.

"You might as well get a shower, son." Dad said. "Mom's going to cook you some breakfast."

"Okay, Pops." I said.

"Annie should be out of there soon." Dad said. "She's getting a lot stronger, isn't she?"

"Yeah." I said. "Maybe in another month she won't need the wheelchair at all."

"Well," Pops said, "You better go check-in on her. She's been in there a good while now. She's your friend, after all."

It suddenly occurred to me that Annie was taking a shower on her own. Something she hadn't done since the accident. Usually, I had to bathe her at least once a week, which was far too seldom, for her liking.

It had consisted of me pouring her a hot bubble bath while she waited in her wheelchair in a pink bathrobe. Then I had to close my eyes as she stripped the robe off her shoulders and I bent to pick her up and set her in the bubble bath. She would then proceed to cover herself with bubbles and take her bath while I sat in her wheelchair and we talked.

It amazed me that we wouldn't have to go through that anymore. After three months Annie was now able to take care of herself for the most part. She'd be able to take a shower daily as she preferred.

I knocked on the bathroom door.

"Everything alright in there?" I asked.

Annie opened the door and pulled me inside.

"We got a problem." She said. "Well, kind of."

"What is it?"

She was in her pink bathrobe and had a white towel done up on her head like a turban.

"It's Miley." She said. "I think I went too far by dancing with him, or something. He's like infatuated with me."

"What?"

"Yeah." She said. "He's been following me around like a little lost puppy."

"Where is he now?" I asked.

"I don't know." She said. "I think he must have finally go the hint and went back to his wife. But after last night and today I wouldn't be surprised if he stuck around. Did you see him out there?"

"No." I said, "I didn't get the chance. I just woke up like 10 minutes ago. I came straight from my room. What happened after I went to sleep?"

"Miley tried to kiss me!" She said. "I told him as best I could that I wasn't into him. Tried to let him down easy but he didn't believe me."

"What did you tell him exactly?"

"Oh, I don't know." Annie sat down in her wheelchair. "I told him I'm not into cops. That I was still grieving over Gerald and the loss of the baby. He won't take no for an answer. He's like stupid or something."

"I'll see if he's still here." I said.

"Wait!" Annie said. "What are you gonna do if he is?"

"I'm gonna tell him to leave you alone." I said.

"That might not work." She said.

"Then I'll threaten him with his job." I said. "Maybe even his wife."

"I don't want you to make a scene." Annie started to cry. "Not in front of your parents! Not on Christmas! What will they think of me for leading him on?"

"It's not like that, Annie."

"They don't know that."

"Look," I said, after a moment. "Let me check to see if he's out there first before you get too upset."

"Tony," She said, as I was about to leave.

"Yeah?"

"What about the money?" She asked. "Did you find a good spot?"

There was a knock at the door.

"Everything okay in there?"

It was dad.

"Yeah," I said. "We're fine. What is it?"

"It's just Annie's breakfast is getting cold."

"I'll be out in a second, Mr. Jackson." Annie said. Despite my dad's insistence that she call him Eugene she always ended up calling him Mr. Jackson. "Is officer Miley still here?" Annie added.

"He took off as soon as you got in the shower." Dad said. "I think he felt uncomfortable around us for some reason. Maybe because we're black and you're a white girl. I don't know. Maybe it was a racial thing. I got some strange vibes about him."

When neither of us responded dad said, “I’ll tell her you’ll be out in a few.”

I listened as dad’s footfalls moved down the hallway towards the kitchen.

“Well,” Annie asked, continuing our conversation. “Did you?”

“I think so.”

“Good.” She said. “Now, take a shower. You stink.”

CHAPTER TWENTY

I closed the door behind Annie as she wheeled out to the kitchen to have breakfast. Briefly, I wondered why she didn’t ask me where I had hid the money. I turned the shower handle and tested the water with my hand, then I got undressed, tested the water again, and hopped in.

I was washing my face with a bar of Irish Spring when I heard the gun popping off. Heard mom scream. Heard a male voice, shouting, “Where is he?”

Another shot.

Silence.

It had to be Ruby.

I turned the faucet handle to the off position as I got out of the shower and cinched a towel around my waist. I wondered where the gun was that I had yesterday. I vaguely remembered leaving it in the hummer while I went to help Nola.

Is that where I left it?

Thinking the cops would protect me?

The golden boy who thwarted the nation’s biggest bank robbery to date and got Delilah Thompson sent to prison after being involved in a shootout with her and her now dead boyfriend, Rob Dickerson, a serial killer and mass murderer, at the bottom of a ravine.

Was I that stupid?

Was my whole family dead?

Even if I got out of this mess the cops weren’t gonna protect me. They were just using me and my family as bait to catch Ruby or whoever else Delilah decided to throw at me. In that moment, I felt that if I were to survive, if my family were to survive and have any peace, I’d have to kill that bitch Delilah.

But how?

I was sure I could contact Mikey. He'd have a Howler or two on the inside that could do away with her.

I thought of all of this as I went to open the door. Knowing that it may be the last time that I did so.

"You coming out, pussy?" Ruby asked, as he tried the knob.

I saw it warble from the other side and lost it.

I wasn't sure if the door was locked or not but it didn't matter. All I could think about was my family lying on the kitchen floor dead. I let out a murderous cry as I flung my body against the door.

All two-hundred-and-forty pounds of it.

The door came off its hinges and plowed into Ruby as he fired his gun and fell against the wall to the floor.

I saw his hand gripping the gun loosely. Unconsciously.

It would only be a moment before he raised it and tried to snuff whoever was on the other side of that door.

Namely me.

I went for the gun. Stepping on his wrist as he cried out in anger and pain.

I thought it was over.

But somehow the door shifted from under me and I slipped and fell, twisting my ankle.

Ruby was quick.

The next thing I knew he was standing over me as I slid my body across the floor like a wounded animal. I raised my hand in self defense, pitifully. I knew it was the end.

I was gonna die naked, holding a towel that was coming loose around my waist.

That's when the inevitable happened.

He lowered the gun and fired and everything went black.

The last words I heard him say were, "I told you I was gonna get you."

Then I died.

I was dead for about twenty minutes before the ambulance came and an EMT got me breathing again. They loaded me up on a stretcher as I asked about my family and covered my mouth with an oxygen mask.

I kept tearing it off to ask about Annie, Mom and Dad. Did they make it?

It must have come out as nothing more than mumbles and moans.

No one answered me.

They just kept telling me that I needed to wear the mask and put it back on every time I tore it off.

Everything went in and out.

I briefly remember being carried out the door and through the yard and being placed in the back of an ambulance. Once inside the medic tried to keep me awake with questions, which only half worked.

"Do you know who did this to you?" He asked.

"It was a hit." I said. "Put out by Delilah Thompson. The hitman's name was Ruby."

"Ruby who?" The medic asked. "What was his last name?"

"Hell if I know!" I said, agitated.

I tore off the oxygen mask again.

"Sir, you need that."

"I don't give a fuck." I said. "Did anyone make it out alive?"

The medic lowered his eyes.

"Tell me goddamn it!" I said.

"We have to worry about you now." He said, and placed the oxygen mask back over my mouth.

At the hospital they put me under anesthesia to take the bullets out of me. When I awoke this time no one was there. Not Annie, not my dad, not my mother, and certainly not Gerald, who'd been dead for some time now.

I had a dream that they were all in heaven. Gerald was on a white steed like some sort of white knight. Annie was on the back looking like a maiden he had rescued, a flower in her hair.

They were all there.

Happy.

Mom was in my dad's arms. They were sitting underneath a large oak tree. Her head and shoulders resting against his chest.

My dad called me over to him as I heard Gerald mumble from his steed, "There's still more to do."

"What is it, pops?" I'd asked. "What is this place?"

He shrugged and told me to look into the river nearby.

I did as I was told.

There I saw my reflection. Years seemed to go by as the reflection changed from that of a fifteen year old boy to a man. Then I saw it.

Ruby's face superimposed on mine.

"So much to do." My mother said, lackadaisically. Even though they were doing nothing but resting by a tree.

Gerald came beside me with his horse and the horse lowered it's head to drink. The ripples washed away the illusion I saw in the river.

"What does it mean?" I asked, turning to Gerald.

My father clapped in time as Annie and my mother laughed and danced. They seemed to be dancing to something upbeat. Although I heard no form of music.

"It means your time hasn't come yet." Gerald said, and smiled.

Then my eyes fluttered open and I was in the hospital. The television was blaring. Andy was teaching Opie how to fish.

I had a flashback of Ruby standing over me with his unmasked, grinning, hair-lip face pointing the gun at me. I was back in the moment again, helpless, wondering if there was anything I could do to get out of the situation. Anyway I could turn it around and win.

If anything I was stubborn, and persistent.

I felt the towel wrapped around my waist, coming loose, as I flung it at him and jumped to my feet. I noticed then that I was standing beside the hospital bed, the towel had not been a towel, but the hospital bedding which I had thrown off me. I was still attached to some of the machines and had felt them tug on my chest and arms as I exploded from the bed.

There was a loud, elongated beep coming from one of the machines. It, and the tug of the machines was, I believe, the only thing that got me to come back from the flashback. I was suffering from some serious PTSD.

Much like a front line marine.

Suddenly, a nurse rushed in and tried to get me settled back on the bed.

Vaguely, I remember asking her if my family was alive.

"Who's your family?" She asked.

“Annie Hankly,” I said, not knowing why I said her name first. “Cynthia and Eugene Jackson.” Mom had kept dad’s last name despite being separated and divorced all those years ago.

“Annie Hankly?” She pondered. “That the short, petite girl with straight, mousy blonde hair?”

I nodded.

“She’s in room 113.”

I shot up from the bed and started ripping the machines’ tentacles off my body. The EKG made a loud, long, high pitched squeal.

“Sir,” The nurse said, trying to push me back onto the bed. “Calm down.”

I slipped the iv out of the crook of my elbow. It spurted with blood. Next thing I knew I was running down the hallway like a madman in a hospital gown.

I came to the end of a cul-de-sac that surrounded a nurses station like a mote. I slapped my hand against the countertop to get the attention of a nurse who was busy looking up at her monitor, typing. She turned her head and stopped typing and looked at me through large Harry Potter type glasses.

“Room 113.” I said, catching my breath. “Where is it?”

She pointed to a room on the other side of the mote.

“Thanks!” I said, and made my way to the room, as the first nurse, the one I had escaped from, ran down the hall shouting after me.

I was stopped by a fat male nurse.

“Only family members may visit.” He said, snidely.

“I am family!” I shouted.

“Relation?” He asked, taking out a clipboard.

“I’m her brother.”

He shook his head. “Half-brother?” He asked, lifting his pen. “Sorry, I just have a hard time believing—.”

“I’m her step-brother.” I said. “I was adopted.”

“I’m sorry.” He said. “You need to be blood relation to visit.”

“You better get out of my way!” I said, and pushed him to the side.

“Tony?” Annie asked, as if waking from a dream. “Is that you?”

"Sir," The first nurse said, finally catching up to me. "She needs her rest. You can't go in there."

She grabbed me by the arm but I shrugged it away and went inside to see how Annie was doing.

"It's me, Annie." I said. "I'm here."

She turned her head to look up at me as I took her hand in mine.

Her head was in bandages. I saw only her left eye peeping out at me as well as her mouth and some tufts of hair. The eye looked dazed and out of it.

I feared the worst.

"Tony." She said, again. Smiling before drifting off and shutting her eye.

"What's wrong with her?" I shouted.

"Nothing's wrong with her." The male nurse said, coming in behind me. "She's on a heavy dose of oxycodone."

"So, she's alright?" I asked.

"As far as I know." He said. "She just needs some rest."

"What's with all the bandages?"

"She fell." The male nurse shrugged.

A doctor came in behind the male nurse.

"Hello," He said. "I'm doctor Jonas."

"I'm Tony." I said, shaking his hand. "I'm her adopted brother. I'm the closest thing she has to a family."

"What would you like to know?" He asked.

"What happened to her?" I asked. "Was she shot? Is she going to be okay?"

"She took a nasty fall." He said. "Hit her head against something hard and got knocked out. My guess is that she was standing instead of sitting in her wheelchair when the perp came in and shot her just below the collar bone. Her legs were weak and wouldn't have been able to keep her on her feet. Heck," He added, "Even if her legs were strong I doubt she would have been able to stay on her feet. Then again the fall might not have been as bad.

"She should be alright though."

"What about my mom and dad?" I asked.

"I believe your dad is in critical condition on the seventh floor. They have done all they can do for him. He has a 50/50 chance of making it."

"And my mom?"

"I'm sorry, Tony." He shook his head.

I ran back down the hallway to the elevators and hit the top button. The elevators were taking too long. So, I took the stairs.

Two floors later I was in the ICU of the hospital on the seventh floor.

I talked to the first person I ran into. A janitor with a mop bucket.

"Excuse me," I said, "Do you know what room Eugene Jackson is in? He's in critical condition. He's my dad."

I had tears in my eyes from the knowledge of my mother being dead but I could hardly mourn her knowing these could be the last moments of my father.

"I believe he's in room 7038." She said, pointing down the hall. "Good luck."

"Thank you." I said, as I rushed down the hallway to room 7038.

This time no one stopped me. I walked right in.

"Pops," I said, as I took his hand.

His eyes blinked open as he turned his head to look at me. His mouth and nose were covered by an oxygen mask.

"Sonny," He said weakly, and smiled.

He never called me that before. Usually it was always Tony or son.

"Listen," He said, barely audible through the mask. "Take this mask off my face so you can hear me. Damnit. I don't have much time."

I did as he said.

"I'm not your real dad." He said.

"What do you mean?" I asked. "Of course you are."

"Listen to me." He said. "I love you as my son. But I never finished telling you what happened once your mom got to the *Verve!* in New York City."

"I'm listening." I said.

"A coward by the name of Jay Lorenzo took pictures of her. He was the sole owner and photographer at *Verve!* at that time. Later, he took her out for drinks. He put something in them. Next thing she knew it was morning and she was in his bed with a headache. He tried to blow things over by cooking breakfast and serving her orange juice. She didn't dare drink or eat anything. Your mother just wanted to leave."

"That doesn't prove that I'm not your son." I said.

"You're mother was a good girl." He added, "She didn't mess around. I met her five months later. When she was pregnant with you." He coughed. "I couldn't help but fall in love with her. I'm sorry, son. It's the truth. Jay Lorenzo is your biological father."

I stood there with tears welled up in my eyes.

"Why didn't she have an abortion?" I asked.

"She didn't believe in it." He said. "Before you were born she believed you were a gift from God. A miracle. Not something Jay had done to her against her consent."

"You mean rape." I said.

Dad nodded.

"We were going to name you Theodore. That's you're real name. Not Tony. It was written on your birth certificate before that nurse, Mrs. Klondike, switched you. Theodore Eugene Jackson." My dad said, proudly. "A fine name for a man. We named you that because it means a 'gift from god.'"

I didn't have the heart to tell him mom was dead. I thought it best if he thought she had survived somehow. I think the old man knew, though.

He could see it in my eyes.

I sat by his side that night holding his hand. I must have fallen asleep because I was awakened by the blare of the machines attached to his body. Nurses rushed in to try to revive him but it was too late.

They had done what they could do.

He was a good man with God now.

Just like mom.

Now, all I had was Annie.

And all Annie had was me.

I went back down the elevator to the fifth floor blinking tears out of my eyes and stayed by Annie's side while she slept.

She awoke sometime before morning as I sat hunched over in a chair half asleep.

"Tony?" She asked.

I lifted my head.

"Yeah?"

"How is everyone?" She asked, weak as a kitten.

"They're dead." I said, wrapping my hands around her hand. "We only have each other now."

"I'm sorry, Tony." She said.

"Yeah, me too." I said, sniffling. "They were as much your family as they were mine. They loved you like a daughter."

"They were like the family I never had." She said.

I didn't have my cell or the card with Mike Scollachi's number on it. They were at the house which was now a crime scene. It wasn't until noon, while I was waiting for my discharge papers, that Officer Miley and his partner came to visit.

Where I was supposed to be discharged to I had no idea.

But eventually they got it all worked out.

I'd be headed for another Hotel paid for by Florida's finest.

But first, I needed that card with Mike Scollachi's number on it.

"I'm real sorry about your mom and dad, kid." Miley said, as they taxi'd me to the crime scene so that I could pick up a few items.

"Yeah," His partner said, "That's a tough one."

His partners name was P. Stinkle. I read it from the tag over his badge. It would have been amusing given any other day. It might have even made me laugh years ago.

When I really was a kid.

You really couldn't get a name worse than that.

I didn't say anything. Too many thoughts and feelings were going through my head. One was anger.

"I'm going to get you, Tony." I heard Ruby's voice saying in my mind, *"You're a dead man."*

And then the gun going off a foot from my chest.

The doctor said I was lucky. Ruby only shot me once. It dawned on me suddenly what the doctor had been trying to convey. That my father, who wasn't really my biological father, took all those bullets for me, mom and Annie.

It just wasn't enough to save mom.

I almost broke down in tears.

He loved me like a son. The only father I ever knew. Gone.

"You alright?" Miley asked, looking at me from his rear-view mirror, as I wiped a tear from my otherwise stoic face.

P. Stinkle turned to me. "Yeah, he's alright." He said, looking me over. "For a kid who lost his parents on Christmas I'd say he's holding up better than average."

Stinkle turned back around.

"Let the kid have his moment, Miley." Stinkle mumbled.

I'm going to kill you, Ruby. I thought, as tears swelled up in my eyes. *If it's the last thing I do. You and Delilah are gonna suffer.*

www.ingramcontent.com/pod-product-compliance
Lightning Source LLC
LaVergne TN
LVHW010558160826
845677LV00013B/3167

* 9 7 9 8 8 4 6 3 3 1 2 5 9 *